The Impact of
Banking Policy on Trade
and Global Stability

The Impact of
Banking Policy on Trade
and Global Stability

NEIL H. ASHDOWN

QUORUM BOOKS
Westport, Connecticut • London

Library of Congress Cataloging-in-Publication Data

Ashdown, Neil H., 1970–
    The impact of banking policy on trade and global stability / Neil H.
Ashdown.
      p. cm.
    Includes bibliographical references and index.
    ISBN 1–56720–522–4 (alk. paper)
    1. Board of Governors of the Federal Reserve System (U.S.) 2. Balance of
payments—United States. 3. Monetary policy—United States. 4. United
States—Commerce. 5. Banks and banking—United States. 6. International
finance. I. Title.
HG2563.A83 2002
337—dc21   2002024804

British Library Cataloguing in Publication Data is available.

Library of Congress Catalog Card Number: 2002024804
ISBN: 1–56720–522–4

First published in 2002

Quorum Books, 88 Post Road West, Westport, CT 06881
An imprint of Greenwood Publishing Group, Inc.
www.quorumbooks.com

Printed in the United States of America

♾™

The paper used in this book complies with the
Permanent Paper Standard issued by the National
Information Standards Organization (Z39.48–1984).

10 9 8 7 6 5 4 3 2 1

Copyright Acknowledgments

The author and publisher are grateful for permission to reproduce material from
the following:

James Livingston, *Origins of the Federal Reserve System: Money, Class, and Corporate Capitalism, 1890–1913* (Ithaca, NY: Cornell University Press, 1986). Reprinted with permission.

Dedicated to Andrea and Roman

Has commerce hitherto done any thing more than change the objects of war? Is not the love of wealth as domineering and enterprising a passion as that of power and glory? Have there not been as many wars founded upon commercial motives since that has become the prevailing system of nations, as were before occasioned by the cupidity of territory or dominion? Has not the spirit of commerce, in many instances, administered new incentives to the appetite, both for the one and for the other?

—Alexander Hamilton, *Federalist No. 6*, 1788

Contents

Acknowledgments   xi

1. Introduction   1
2. Institutional versus Realist Models   7
3. Banking on the Fed for a Healthy Economy   27
4. The Cultural Evolution of Institutions in the United
   States   55
5. Monetary Policy, Foreign Exchange, and Trade   79
6. Final Thoughts   109

Appendix A: Exhibits   117
Appendix B: The Research Design   123
Notes   129
References   133
Index   139

Acknowledgments

There are many people that I must thank, because without them this work could never have come to fruition. Judith Gillespie at the University at Albany, State University of New York, spent countless hours editing and encouraging me when the end was nowhere in sight. Her intellect, expertise, merciless red pen, and boundless energy were invaluable to the entirety of this work.

Professor Robert Nakamura was also very influential in helping me understand the important role that policy, or the lack of it, plays in the world. His keen mind was always making me ask the tough questions that I did not always want to ask.

I am very grateful to Mim Vasan, John Donohue, and everyone at Greenwood Publishing Group. They guided me through the publication process with professionalism and patience.

There were many other scholars, policy makers, colleagues, and acquaintances along the way whose input and advice, while not always heeded, was greatly appreciated.

I am extremely grateful to Ed Winders, whose generous gift established the Joseph F. Zimmerman Fellowship at the Graduate School of Public Affairs and Policy at the University at Albany, State University of New York. I was honored to be named the first Zimmerman Fellow, and Mr. Winders' generosity assisted me with the research expenses associated with my doctoral research.

I must also thank the many elected and appointed officials, bankers, financial analysts, brokers, public auditors, and the people at the Federal Reserve Bank of New York, in particular, who helped me find documents and offered insight.

I would like to thank my parents, Laurence and Diane Ashdown, who instilled in me the importance of an education, and my grandfather, Hazen Cooley, whose dedication to higher education first inspired me to attend graduate school.

I would like to thank Mario and Sara Zullo for understanding why I needed to take their daughter so far away from home, and for not asking why I was dedicating so many years of my life to a career that satisfies my intellectual curiosity but does not pay very well.

Most of all, I must thank my wife, Andrea, who over the years has put up with all of the late nights on the computer and apartments, homes, and hotel rooms scattered with piles of books and chapter drafts. Through it all she has been supportive and understanding, and without her encouragement this work would never have been possible.

The Impact of
Banking Policy on Trade
and Global Stability

Chapter 1

Introduction

The world has become increasingly more globally interdependent as nation-states have grown dependent on foreign trade and investment to sustain their standard of living. The global marketplace for trade has expanded, and along with it, global trade policy has grown in importance for the majority of the world's most industrialized countries. The United States consistently runs a trade deficit. The U.S. trade deficit is causing the American standard of living to become increasingly dependent on foreign investment to finance the deficit, while many other industrialized countries, such as Germany or Japan, consistently run trade surpluses, or at the very least, manage a trade balance. The differences among these countries may very well lie in their fiscal and monetary policies, particularly in regard to trade issues.

The research question that this study addresses is: Why has the United States not actively pursued policies to create trade balances or surpluses in recent years? The study will test whether direct linkages between central banking monetary policies and national trade deficits or surpluses exist, with specific emphasis on the U.S. Federal Reserve System, and why policy makers should or should not concern themselves with trade imbalances in an increasingly economically interdependent world. The United States is the country analyzed in the case study, with pertinent comparisons being made to Germany when comparative analysis is helpful in explaining monetary policy or trade policy in relation to institutional power. The independent and dependent variable relationships that may fall under this scenario will be examined closely, including historical occurrences that may directly influence the monetary policies of capitalist societies and the percentage of gross domestic product (GDP) that is produced, as well as what effect that has on the central banking authorities when creating monetary policy.

This study examines the hypothesis that trade deficits are caused by specific U.S. policies which guide the monetary policies of the Federal Reserve System. In the following pages the findings of each chapter are briefly outlined, with the refutable premise that institutions do matter, both within the domestic policymaking circles of nation-states and in the international policy arena, standing as the most glaring deviance from neorealist theory.

Under a neorealist balance of power model, institutions are merely tools of the state, and therefore actions of these institutions are merely policies acting for and on behalf of the national interest, or are inconsequential in the larger national policy sphere. Most foreign and economic policy is generated in the highest circles according to the theoretical parameters of neorealist models; therefore, one of the most powerful U.S. institutions, and one of the world's most influential organizations, the U.S. Federal Reserve System, should be acting not only in concert with the best interests of the nation-state, but actually acting as a tool of the nation-state. Therefore, a case study of the U.S. Federal Reserve System, both as a tool of the U.S. government and as an institution with international influence, examined through the neorealist lense, should prove that if indeed Fed policies cause trade deficits, then trade deficits must somehow be in the national interest, or at least play a minor role in the larger scheme of things. This study concludes otherwise, and that in fact institutions do matter, as the Federal Reserve often constrains national policy, rather than reacts to it.

I then looked at the data under the institutional model, which is the main competing theory in international relations, to see if there were alternative explanations or if other factors were at play. The results of this study could have found that Fed policy is in support of the national interest and that its policies purposefully strengthen the U.S. militarily, thus giving substance to the neorealist paradigm, or it could have found that the Fed is acting in concert with the nation's economic interests, without regard to the nation's military might, which would fall more in line with the institutional model.

The study could also have found that the Fed is acting on behalf of its own interests as an institution, which would again best be supported by the institutional model; or it could have found that Fed policies are not beneficial to the institution or the nation, but instead to only a small group of international financiers, thus invalidating the two mainstream theories, possibly requiring alternative approaches altogether, such as the ideas or constructivist approaches.

Chapter 2 of this study briefly identifies and analyzes the relative literature surrounding the two main paradigms in international relations, institutional and neorealist models. The content of that chapter will lay the groundwork for the main concepts and ideas that will be used to analyze and answer the research question.

Chapter 3 will identify and defend the reasoning behind looking at this research project through the lenses of U.S. banking, and particularly the institution that serves as the lender of last resort for the United States, the U.S. Federal Reserve System. The relevance of banking in international trade was debated in years past, and recently has sparked interest once again in international political economy circles as new evidence has been developed that demonstrates its importance even in antiquity.

The next several chapters will identify the actual trade research. Chapter 4 will begin the case study of U.S. banking, and then the following chapter will provide an in-depth look at the Fed's policies. The first goal will be to outline the goals and objectives of the U.S. Federal Reserve System and to look at interest rate management practices and monetary policy specifically. Federal Reserve publications and web sites were used as sources to outline the institution's objectives and mission according to its own definitions, and then the author's own analysis of the Federal Reserve's policies is used to critique and to supplement the documentation.

The goal of Chapter 4 is to take a look at why the U.S. Federal Reserve System came into existence. An analysis of the relevant academic literature on this subject was undertaken to provide a thorough understanding of how the Federal Reserve System became the institution it is today and why the corporate capitalists of the nineteenth and twentieth centuries believed such an institution was essential to a trading society. A historical approach demonstrates what factors led to the emergence of a central bank in the United States and which group or groups gained an advantage by its creation.

Understanding how the Federal Reserve came into existence will shed some light on roles that institutions may play in achieving the interests of specific groups versus the national interest.

Chapter 5 continues by identifying German Bundesbank objectives, with the main purpose being to demonstrate how the two systems, U.S. and German, deal with the issue of trade. Data for this section was drawn from a variety of sources, including governmental and nongovernmental statistics, web sites and institutional publications, academic research, and studies from a variety of policy institutes and think tanks.

Once the objectives of the two banking systems have been outlined, the data on international trade for the two countries will be displayed and analyzed primarily for the decade leading up to the official integration of the European Monetary Union and the establishment of the euro as the currency for the EMU on January 1, 1999. An analysis of the trade data demonstrates how central bank policies affected the surplus/deficit ratios of the two countries. This analysis allows conclusions to be drawn regarding which areas of the economy—unemployment, inflation, foreign investment, and exchange rates—the central banks considered more important, and presumably in the national interest. The comparison in this section serves mainly to demonstrate how two systems that are so similar in purpose and disciplined in rigid monetary policies can have such different trade results.

In Chapter 6 the findings of the study are summarized, specifically as to how institutions help groups meet their objectives, and often drive the objectives of entire nation-states. The study demonstrates how institutions have become important international actors in the global economy and have changed the balance of power in the international system.

Critiques of this study will point out various weaknesses with my approach, particularly from two main standpoints. First, the subnational unit of analysis at first glance seems to be deductive, thus providing a weak test to the systemic theory that neorealism offers; and second, there is a bias factor that accompanies the case study approach. My answer to these criticisms is that the case study of the U.S. system should not be viewed as a detrimental factor because while the results of the actual study may not be generalizable to the international system—because I do acknowledge that the bias factor exists with the case study approach, where a study can be chosen that fits a predetermined hypothesis—it is the theory that I am test-ing. The conclusion that I walk away with from this study—that institutions do matter both in domestic and international policy-making arenas—is generalizable. Theories can be made generalizable from subsets to the larger system without the deductive problems that come with trying to make data generalizable from the part to the whole.

As far as using the United States, and then studying the banking system, and ultimately the Federal Reserve System as the institution for this study, again the bias factor cannot be ignored where I may have picked an institution that fits my hypothesis. The United States has been declared by many as the military, and even the economic hegemon of the post-bipolar world. Central banks, in an era where liquidity and credit are so vital to commerce, are compelling forces that help drive and regulate the economic machines of nation-states. The U.S. Federal Reserve System, being the central bank of the last remaining superpower to survive the Cold War era, and certainly one of the most influential players in the world, was chosen because of its influence in the United States and the world. The timeliness of such a study is no accident, given the fact that, at the time this study was conducted, I lived in the United States and in the state of New York, home of the Federal Open Market Committee, the monetary policymaking arm of the Federal Reserve.

In my defense, I must state that when I originally decided to take on this study, I started out to prove that Waltz's structural balance of power theory could still be applied in the modern international system, as long as the power focus was shifted away from military might to economic pervasiveness and influence. I walked away from the study still thinking that this theory could have explanatory value within certain parameters, but that the most important finding to take away is that institutions do matter and that they shape and constrain policy, sometimes in the national interest and sometimes not, but nearly always in the interest of the group that the institution represents.

Some of the findings of this study are more in the tradition of scholarship that (a) points out that a specific policy failed to support the national interest, (b) looks at why the policy failed, and (c) ad-vocates an alternative policy which better supports the national in-terest. This work predates the neorealist, Waltzian formulations, not expecting government institutions to always support the national interest, yet not dismissing the neorealist premise of a national interest.

Whether or not the United States is a hegemon and whether economics has fully surpassed military might—or whether military might ever was the real core of national power—is touched on in this study. But these are certainly topics for further study, as I have only scratched the surface of these topics here.

Chapter 2

Institutional versus Realist Models

DEFINING TRADE AND TRADE DEFICITS

When we hear about trade in the media, quite often the topic concerns the current account. While the current account factors in trade, the current account deficit is not the same as the trade deficit. The current account calculates all payments and receipts from abroad. Besides net exports, the current account also includes dividends, social security checks paid out to retired U.S. citizens living abroad, and forms of aid or grants. Prior to the early 1980s, the United States had seldom run significant current account deficits. However, beginning in about 1983, the United States began to consistently compile annual deficits, with the exception of a period in the early 1990s (the current account deficit tends to decrease in recessionary years, due largely to a slowdown in imported goods). In recent years, the trade portion of the current account deficit has garnered the most attention. The trade deficit, occuring when a country imports more goods and services than it exports, is the portion of the current account deficit that this study will look at.

The U.S. trade deficit became more noteworthy in 1996 when a trend in slowing exports began. This new trend was a cause for concern because traditionally the trade deficit in the United States did not stem from exporting too little; it derived from importing too much.

THE IMPORTANCE OF TRADE DEFICITS

When Bill Clinton was first elected president, he indicated that he would take on the trade deficit problem, even make it one of the priorities of his administration. Despite this goal, however, the trade deficit actually reached record levels during the 1990s, rising nearly every year Clinton was in office. Of course, the decade of the 1990s was one of the brightest decades in U.S. history when measured in terms of economic growth, so what happened during that time period that caused the trade deficit to rise? Stagnant productivity levels in the United States caused the trade deficit gap to increase in the late 1980s and early 1990s, while economic wealth and the increasing strength of the dollar caused the gap to widen further in the late 1990s as Americans imported foreign goods as never before. The strong U.S. dollar priced American goods out of reach in most markets abroad, so even though the U.S. economy was booming, the rate of growth for exports was slowing.

There are many economists and policy makers who do not see trade deficits in the United States as a cause for concern, largely because exports comprise a small portion of the U.S. GDP, generally in the 10 to 12 percent range. This fact is one of the main reasons that monetary policy to combat trade deficits has not been addressed. In many industrialized countries, central banking policy is aimed at governing inflation. If the central banking authority stands by monetarist strategies that merely regulate the economy through anti-inflationary measures, then moves to erase trade deficits would not generally be a primary goal since devaluing the currency is the most effective way of erasing deficits. Devaluing the currency is, for all intents and purposes, a prescription for inflation, the very antithesis of the monetarist strategy. Many developing countries, such as Argentina or Brazil, along with several OECD (Organization for Economic Cooperation and Development) countries, such as Japan and Germany, depend more heavily on exports to sustain their economies. Therefore, it makes sense for these countries to have central banking policies that target trade surpluses, or, at the very minimum, trade balances.

The small percentage that exports add to the U.S. GDP should not be trivialized, however. It would be hard to imagine the damage losing 10 to 12 percent of a country's GDP would do to its economy. Another important factor to consider is the seriousness of the trend.

As I mentioned earlier, until the early 1980s the United States seldom ran current account deficits, yet since then it has consistently run deficits and has had to finance that debt to foreign countries to sustain its standard of living. Each year that percentage has risen, and it does not look as if that trend will be reversed. Furthermore, jobs that stem from international exports are higher paying than average domestic jobs, and exports actually comprise a substantial portion of U.S. economic growth when measured in value, even though they represent a small percentage of the economy as a whole.

These facts alone would make one stop and wonder why the United States would not be concerned with the trade deficit, not to mention foreign financing of the debt, which could lead to other major problems such as isolationist policies due to perceived threats to national security.

Why don't policy makers in the United States concern themselves with trade deficits, especially since trade is increasing in importance for the overall health of the economy? The answer is certainly multifaceted; however, a major part of the technical solution to this enigma is that the central banking authority focuses on anti-inflationary monetary policies while excluding from its list of objectives an active role in maintaining a balance of trade.

THE CASE STUDY

This study originates from a U.S. perspective and uses the case study of the U.S. banking system as the research design. While the study originates from a U.S. perspective, Germany, especially prior to integration within the European Monetary Union (EMU), has many striking similarities that make it attractive for comparisons, particularly in Chapter 5. Both nations are major players in the economic and international trade arenas, and both countries' central banks have actively been engaged in monetary policy strategies that have concentrated on inflation-fighting measures for the last several decades.

The area where Germany and the United States differ dramatically, and that gives the trade data analysis a valuable comparative policy bent in Chapter 5, is that the German Bundesbank has also implemented into its objectives the matter of promoting trade, and has done this effectively. The U.S. Federal Reserve, on the other hand, has not been actively concerned with promoting policies that would reduce trade deficits. In fact, I would argue that the Fed's strict inflation-fighting mechanisms have perpetuated annual trade deficits. U.S. policy makers push for a dollar that is valued very high on the exchange rate market, making it a viable target for foreign investment. The monetary policy is often so rigid that even in times of crisis the Fed refuses to devalue the dollar. To its credit, the Fed has made other important and timely moves rather than devaluation when the nation needed its leadership to keep the economy afloat. One such move occurred after the terrorist attacks on the World Trade Center and the Pentagon on September 11, 2001, when the Fed flooded the markets with liquidity to keep commerce flowing and ATM machines full, demonstrating its ability to lead and act as a calming agent in times of crisis.

Germany understands the importance of global trade, as the health of its economy has depended on it for decades, or arguably even centuries. It ran annual surpluses throughout much of the decade of the 1990s, in spite of other real fiscal and monetary policy concerns occupying the country's attention such as the reunification process with East Germany and preparations to meet rigid budgetary requirements for the EMU.

A German embassy brief on the economic structure of the nation released around the mid 1990s even as Germany was preparing for economic integration, stated, "The goal is to ensure price stability, high employment levels and a stable trade balance while maintaining steady and adequate economic growth" (U.S. Department of State, September 1996). Even as Germany was making tough choices in order to keep its budget within the Maastricht Treaty parameters that were required for EU member countries integrating their currencies and banking systems by 1999, it was still targeting a trade balance as one of its main objectives.

The Bundesbank demonstrated its commitment to a positive trade balance by keeping tight controls over the value of the deutsche mark. For example, when the dollar was temporarily undermined by the crisis in Mexico at the end of 1994 and pervasive economic turmoil embroiled Europe, the Bundesbank witnessed a massive increase in deutsche mark investment as countries began pouring their funds into deutsche marks instead of dollars. The Bundesbank quickly took action in 1995 by easing back on their monetary policy to provide for a devaluation of the currency (U.S. Treasury, January 15, 1996). The move slowed the economic growth rate and had some lingering effects in regards to an increase in the unemployment rate; but even with the policy decision to devalue, the rate of inflation remained far below the German target parameters of 2 percent (U.S. Treasury, January 15, 1996).

The United States and Germany are two of the most instrumental players in the world's economy. Both countries have (or had in the case of Germany, as much of Germany's monetary policy is now conducted from the European Central Bank) central banking institutions that engage in rigid anti-inflationary monetary policies; yet when comparing trade data, the congruencies between these two countries dissolve. Germany's central bank, prior to unification, was an autonomous institution with a clear policy objective to engage in active trade policy. The U.S. Federal Reserve, on the other hand, with no clear trade policy objectives and rigid monetary policies toward inflation, helps perpetuate the massive trade deficits in the United States.

It seems evident that the similarities of these two countries' central banking systems, and their anti-inflationary techniques in particular, make the data comparisons in Chapter 5 a good fit for this type of analysis. It allows for an added layer of data gathering rigor through the testing of a case study within a case study research design, specifically by comparing German data to the U.S. case study research model. Because one country consistently runs trade deficits while the other achieves surpluses (and their central banking policies are directly linked to these phenomena), the case study approach is a strong method for explaining why some countries actively pursue policies that create trade balances or surpluses, while others do not.

PARADIGMS AND LITERATURE

Why do some countries actively promote policies that create trade balances or surpluses while others do not? There are economic and theoretical arguments on both sides of the issue, ranging from Keynesianism to Chicago school free market arguments on the economic front and rational actor to institutional arguments in international relations theory. Most U.S. policies in regard to the economy are founded on free market principles and rational actor theories.

Economists' opinions range all over the map on the subject of trade. Some, like Milton Friedman, argue that the market should be left alone when it comes to trade policy and that monetary policies should only be concerned with technical issues, such as achieving monetary targets in order to achieve a steady growth of the money supply. Friedman's advice would indicate that a central banking authority should not involve itself in creating trade policy. There are other economists and policy makers who feel that the Fed should be actively engaged in promoting a trade balance, and then there are those who don't believe the trade deficit is a problem at all. Paul Krugman, a renowned economist from MIT, has stated that while the arguments over the seriousness of the trade deficit have supporters on both sides, all economists agree on one major aspect: "The trade deficit does have a cost: a gradual mortgaging of future U.S. income to foreigners" (Krugman, 1995:48). If Krugman's statement is viewed as correct, and I believe that it is, it would seem to belie any strategy that does not promote trade balances, yet the United States does not actively pursue such a policy.

Why would any country that is acting as a "rational actor" in a market-structured economy allow its future to be mortgaged to foreigners? Under the rational actor paradigm, allowing one nation-state to have power over another through such a dependency as a trade deficit provides does not seem to fit the model. Both classical liberal economics and realism, or neorealism—the mainstream theories in the respective fields of economics and international relations upon which nearly all current policy is based—rely on rational actor models. It will prove beneficial then, in this section, to recognize other factors that may play into the formula; and theoretical debates will be explored that may refute the rational actor model in the trade deficit issue. It is fairly obvious that central banking policies correlate to a country's trade deficits, so it would seem to be more important to understand why a country's central bank does or does not attempt to maintain a balance of trade.

Understanding these phenomena will help us understand the larger question of why some countries' policy makers are more concerned with trade deficits than others. In the classical economic sense, it does seem that what Weimer and Vining term market failure has occurred in relation to the U.S. trade deficit. It would seem that an active trade policy that pursued, at the very least, a balance of trade would be in the best interests of the country. Weimer and Vining in fact argue that if Pareto efficiency is not occurring—meaning when it "would not be possible for anyone to find a reallocation that would make at least one person better-off without making at least one person worse-off," (Weimer and Vining, 1992:31)—then this is a situation where collective action, government policy intervention, may improve the efficiency ratio and enhance the good of the nation. This contradiction will be examined at a later point, but there may be structural effects that keep U.S. trade policy heading in the same direction, which I will argue stem from institutional constraints.

In methodological terms, the main research models that will be examined in this literature review deal with the ongoing debate between the rational-actor models and the institutional model. Because I am interested in trade as it pertains to international relations, it is prudent to develop Kenneth Waltz's "balance-of-power theory" that stems from his book *A Theory of International Politics*. Kenneth Waltz's neorealist theory is still the dominant rational actor theory studied and used today in international relations, and in fact the largest portion of scholarly work performed in the field since Waltz wrote his book in 1979 has either been intended to supplement his work or to critique it.

Waltz defines his balance-of-power theory by using, as both classical realists and neorealists do, a systemic approach. Waltz defines systems theories as explaining

how the organization of a realm acts as a constraining and disposing force on the interacting units within it. . . . To the extent that dynamics of a system limit the freedom of its units, their behavior and the outcomes of their behavior become predictable. (Waltz, 1979:60)

Neorealists tend to approach nation-states as the main point of focus within the international system. Waltz then goes on to suggest that the way these nation-states relate to one another, in accordance to the relative power of each, is a structural effect. The structure of the system then will define the relationship of the units in where they stand in the international system. It is prudent to insert here Waltz's definition of structure.

Structure is not something we see. . . . To define a structure requires ignoring how units relate with one another (how they interact) and concentrating on how they stand in relation to one another (how they are arranged or positioned). (Waltz, 1979:71–72)

Waltz builds from Emile Durkheim's discourse on how mechanical societies transform into organic societies through a necessity of survival. At a unit level Durkheim states that individuals come

sufficiently in contact to be able to act and react upon one another. If we agree to call this relation and the active commerce resulting from it dynamic or moral density, we can say that the progress of the division of labor is in direct ratio to the moral or dynamic density of society. (Durkheim, 1964: 257)

Waltz transposes this theory into international relations theory by associating nation-states, which are by his definition self-help actors, to societies that move from a mechanical to an organic structure. Waltz emphatically states that "only a structural transformation can abolish the international imperative—take care of yourself!—and replace it with the domestic one—specialize!" (Keohane, 1986:326).

Robert O. Keohane has critiqued Waltz's structural theory by assuming that in Waltz's theory states must seek to maximize power in order to fit into a systemic theory. Keohane compares this idea to microeconomic theory, stating:

Both use the rationality assumption to permit inferences about actor behavior to be made from system structure. The Realist definition of interests in terms of power and position is like the economist's assumption that firms seek to maximize profits: it provides the utility function of the actor. Through these assumptions, actor characteristics become constant rather than variable, and systemic theory becomes possible. (Keohane, 1986:167)

In fact, Kenneth Waltz may not necessarily subscribe to this notion in the way that Keohane has described, posing instead that states will seek enough power for their own particular needs, not necessarily to maximize them. Waltz has used microeconomic theory to explain his theory, but it only works for power maximizing actors. A better comparison for Keohane could possibly have been to a nonprofit organization, where Harold J. Seymour explains that "financial support has to be there, and indeed on an ever-increasing scale, but never at the cost of independence or integrity of purpose or program" (Seymour, 1988:19). Waltz explains this principal further when he formally refutes Keohane's statements, saying:

Keohane rightly criticizes some realists for assuming that states seek to maximize power. He wrongly associates me with them because I point out that a balance-of-power system works whether we find states seeking only the minimum of power needed for security or whether some of them strive for domination. (Keohane, 1986:334)

Therefore, it is clear from Waltz's statements that he does not believe that power is an end in itself, but purely a means to an end. The degree that each nation-state attempts to achieve power depends on its ultimate motives. Some nation-states, therefore, may attempt to maximize power because they are seeking domination, while others may have ulterior motives, such as higher standard-of-living levels, but need to achieve a certain level of power in order to be able to safely go about accomplishing their higher motives. This situation is where the nonprofit organization is a better fit to Waltz's theory than the microeconomic theory of the firm that Keohane introduces. Whereas a firm does seek to maximize its profit, and perpetuating its own survival is its ultimate goal, the nonprofit organization seeks profits so that it can remain solvent, therefore allowing it to seek its main purpose, such as finding a cure for cancer or finding shelter for the homeless.

Keohane's allusion to the firm is not altogether lost however, because a microeconomic theory of the firm is useful in describing how socialization and competitiveness occur in a structure. An example will provide a nice segue to our next topic. Firms, whether profit-maximizing or nonprofit, still must remain competitive in order to stay solvent. Waltz explains that

competitive systems are regulated, so to speak, by the "rationality" of the more successful competitors. What does rationality mean? It means only that some do better than others—whether through intelligence, skill, hard work, or dumb luck. They succeed in providing a wanted good or service more attractively and more cheaply than others do. Either their competitors emulate them or they fall by the wayside. . . . Those who survive share certain characteristics. Those who go bankrupt lack them. Competition spurs the actors to accommodate their ways to the socially most acceptable and successful practices. (Waltz, 1979:66)

It is at this line of thinking where I will deviate from traditional forms of power—meaning military strength—and shift to the "new" form of power—economic—which is where I believe the new system is being shaped by a shift in the power structure. Waltz, along with most other neorealists and realists, have long argued that economic power is secondary to military power, and it is here that Keohane and the institutionalists provide a better argument than the realists to explain the post–Cold War era.

I should insert here that when discussing the institutionalists, I am also including international organizational theorists with this group. There are minor differences in the two fields, but for my purpose they can be categorized under the subheading of institutionalists.

Institutionalism essentially accepts the realist notion of an anarchic system, meaning that there is no single enforcing agency or governing body for the entire international system, but institutionalists believe that there are other important actors within the system besides nation-states, such as regimes, international organizations, and corporations. They also hold, realists would argue idealistically, that cooperation within the international system is possible and that there does not have to be a zero-sum game—all parties can have a positive gain.

The fundamental difference between the institutionalists and the organizational theorists is that the organizationalists believe that once an organization is created, it will try to promote its continued existence but will resist change and attempt to enforce the status quo. The institutionalists would argue that organizations will try to shift their focus while using existing norms and regimes to hold it together, but that organizations will reconfigure or change goals in order to ensure survival.

Realists would support the idea that under a uni-polar world, such as some critics claim we live in now, the system would change from an anarchy to a hierarchy, and this scenario could not occur for extended periods of time in a pure neorealist theory. However, it can be argued that due to the collapse of the Soviet empire, the structure of the system began to shift in order to fill the void in the bipolar system. Some political scientists have argued that due to the collapse of the bipolar system, there is more anarchy now than ever before. John J. Mearsheimer (1990) argued in "Back to the Future: Instability in Europe after the Cold War" that a shift in the structure following a collapse of the bipolar power structure would be far more chaotic than under the bipolar system that the world witnessed throughout the Cold War. He stated:

I argue that the prospects for major crises and war in Europe are likely to increase markedly if the Cold War ends and this scenario unfolds. The next decades in a Europe without the superpowers would probably not be as violent as the first 45 years of this century, but would probably be substantially more prone to violence than the past 45 years.

This pessimistic conclusion rests on the argument that the distribution and character of military power are the root causes of war and peace. Specifically, the absence of war in Europe since 1945 has been a consequence of three factors: the bipolar distribution of military power on the Continent; the rough military equality between the two states comprising the two poles in Europe, the United States and the Soviet Union; and the fact that each superpower was armed with a large nuclear arsenal. (Mearsheimer, 1990:6)

It would not be beneficial for the United States to attack another country, for example, if that country refused to trade freely with the United States or allow U.S. corporations to locate plants and branches within its borders. First, such an attack might (a) incite other nations to punish the United States for its aggression by not trading with them either, or (b) inspire new alliances to form against the United States, thus changing the power structure in the international system in a way that would not benefit the United States. Neither response would be in the interest of the United States. Mearsheimer stated that "this competitive world is peaceful when it is obvious that the costs and risks of going to war are high, and the benefits of going to war are low" (Mearsheimer, 1990:12).

The point can possibly be better understood through the analysis of the one nation-state that is said to be standing alone in the new international system, the United States. Durkheim argued that as societies become more specialized, they grow increasingly dependent on one another (Durkheim, 1964). Waltz argued the same point by stating that "the division of labor brings unlikes together" (Keohane, 1986:325). Is this not exactly what has happened in the new global economy?

Paul Krugman promoted the idea that the standard of living in America was growing increasingly dependent on the investments of foreign nation-states (Krugman, 1995). The political scientist Donald M. Snow posed the idea that among Americans there is a growing concern that as the standard of living in the United States grows more reliant on foreign investments, the role of the United States as a superpower is perceived to be decreasing in the international community (Snow, 1995). This notion is important because as the U.S. debt grows larger, it is forced to either borrow or allow other nation-states the opportunity to invest further. This economic dependency may hinder the United States from going to war and using its military prowess, thus creating the new balance of power within the international system. It is important to note that realists would never agree with this scenario because they do not accept the notion that economic power could rival military power. In fact, the reality that a rational actor theory can be adapted to fit nearly any scenario, and that it is difficult to empirically test, is one of the major criticisms of the realist paradigm.

It is important to note that the United States is not only growing increasingly dependent on international financing, but foreigners now hold large asset portfolios in the United States that have a tremendous influence on the U.S. economy. As foreigners increase their U.S. asset portfolios, foreign governments will have more power in the international system. Under this scenario the structure of the system may actually shift, as the balance-of-power theory would indicate, not due to a rising military threat, but instead to an institutional threat. Many critics of this theory rightly question whether foreign-held assets within the United States actually give these countries the power over the United States that this theory implies, and instead if it might not actually be possible for the United States to gain power over the investing states by threatening to seize or otherwise hinder their enjoyment of these assets.

While this scenario is valid in theory—and has taken place on a smaller scale in practice, such as during the Gulf War, when Iraqi accounts were frozen—it would be highly unlikely for the international community to cooperate with such a move against any of the industrialized countries, which are the main players in this structural shift. The United States has spoken out against any form of nationalization of private industries, like those in South America during the last century, and would not likely contradict its own policy by carrying out the same policies it harshly criticized before.

The example noted above demonstrates that the United States is not a lone hegemon that can act freely without consequences and demonstrates that institutions such as trade agreements and security organizations, which the United States has endorsed, are now actually constraining the policies and actions of the United States.

Therefore, if the international system is a system made up of units struggling for their own survival through self-interested actions, or a system of self-help, then the United States is not the lone super-power some envision it to be, but perhaps only an actor within an institutional framework. Kenneth Waltz states that:

An international-political system is one of self-help. In a self-help system, states are differently placed by their power. States are self-regarding units. State behavior varies more with differences of power than with differences in ideology, in internal structure of property relations, or in governmental form. (Keohane, 1986:329)

If, in fact, the United States is not the lone hegemonic power at the top of some hierarchical order, then what are the other units that have stepped up to rival the power of the United States in accordance with this self-help philosophy and create the continuity of anarchy that is so vital to a balance-of-power theory? Giovanni Arrighi writes in his book *The Long Twentieth Century* that:

Superiority of force and the capitalist accumulation of capital seemed to diverge geopolitically as never before. The decline of Soviet power was matched by the emergence of what Bruce Cumings has aptly called the "capitalist archipelago" of East and Southeast Asia. This archipelago consists of several "islands" of capitalism, which rise above a "sea" of horizontal exchanges among local and world markets through the centralization within their domains of large-scale profits and high value-added activities. . . . Collectively, the competitiveness of the East and Southeast Asian capitalist archipelago as the new "workshop of the world" is the single most important factor forcing the traditional centers of capitalist power—Western Europe and North America—to restructure and reorganize their own industries, their own economies, and their own ways of life. (Arrighi, 1994:22)

It is certain that Arrighi would argue that the collective economic forces of East and Southeast Asian countries would comprise some form of a new unit that was reshaping the structure of the international system. During the last several years this part of the world has been struggling, but it is unclear whether their woes are structural or cyclical. Along these same lines, it could be argued that the European Union, as it continues down the path of economic integration, would also be a potential unit struggling for one of the "power positions" within the anarchic structural order of the international system. Robert Keohane, Joseph Nye, and Stanley Hoffman (1993) argue in *After the Cold War* that international organizations, or institutions, often shape nation-state policy. When the world system is looked at through this set of lenses, it makes sense of the new trend in forming international trade blocs that consequently are not unlike the military alliances forged under previous structures. Moreover, this economic interdependency can be viewed as the specialization of labor that Waltz discusses when analyzing Durkheim's views of how mechanical societies develop into organic societies. Waltz explains Durkheim's concept more thoroughly by stating that:

A mechanical society rests on the similarity of the units that compose it; an organic society is based on their differences. An organic society promotes the sharpening of individual talents and skills. Different parts of the society make their particular contributions to its general welfare. Units become closely linked because they do special jobs and then exchange goods and services in order to meet their common requirements. The division of labor increases efficiency and promotes the general prosperity. (Keohane, 1986:324–325)

This concept takes on a real meaning for students of the world economy. Donald Snow asserts that:

The world is increasingly one in which all nations are forced to rely upon one another for a variety of goods and services. This phenomenon is known as *interdependence*, the mutual dependence of all nations on other nations for their well-being and, in some cases, survival. The First Tier nations rely on the Second Tier for energy and mineral resources necessary to run their industrial plants, and the Second Tier depends on the developed nations for industrial and agricultural goods. Proponents of the interdependence school maintain that this mutual dependence is increasing and that, in the future, the nations of the world will come to depend on one another to such an extent that it will not be possible for them to come into violent conflict. (Snow, 1995:31)

The idea of economic power surpassing the role of military power and shifting structural forces due to policies formulated in response to global interdependency is not an idea that balance-of-power theorists would endorse. There are critics out there who, of course, claim that the United States has become a hegemonic power in the international system and is therefore not interdependent. Some have even countered the economic argument by claims that, while foreign investment is growing within the United States, it is still not a large factor in the U.S. economy.

An article written by Laura D'Andrea Tyson suggests that the outlook is not nearly as grim as some analysts might suggest. She writes that "foreign affiliates, whatever their character, still represent a relatively small fraction of total economic activity within the United States" (Tyson, 1991:4). This statement may be somewhat misleading, however. While it is true that the largest portion of U.S. GNP is still produced by companies within the borders of the United States, that percentage is rapidly falling, and the prospect of removing foreign financial support would be staggering. The real story is not the "relatively small fraction" that Laura D'Andrea Tyson speaks of, but rather it is the trend that must be studied.

The U.S. debt burden to its foreign investors has steadily increased over the last several years, as measured as a percentage of GDP. Clearly the trend is moving in a direction that needs to be looked at closely and not merely trivialized as a banal anomaly.

Critics of this unit-level example may be tempted to call this analysis a move away from systemic theory and more of a description using a reductionist theory. However, this criticism would be inaccurate primarily because I am not showing how the actions of the United States have reshaped the system. It is merely a case study that illustrates how institutions may be shaping the ways nation-states create policy, in contradiction to realist notions that institutions are tools of the nation-state. It would not be logical from many viewpoints for the United States to allow its trade deficit, for instance, to be financed by foreigners, from a national security point of view. This analysis may be an example of how the United States, a unit-level actor, is being coerced, or at the very least constrained, in its actions.

Waltz agrees that there may be other forces constraining the actions of states, but that it is the structural influence of the system that is doing the constraining. He states:

Each state arrives at policies and decides on actions according to its own internal processes, but its decisions are shaped by the very presence of other states as well as by interactions with them. (Waltz, 1979:52–53)

Furthermore, within that system there is the structure that makes up that system. Under specific structures, the units within that structure behave differently.

Agents and agencies act; systems as a whole do not. But the actions of agents and agencies are affected by the system's structure. In itself a structure does not directly lead to one outcome rather than another. Structure affects behavior within the system, but does so indirectly. The effects are produced in two ways: through socialization of the actors and through competition among them. (Waltz, 1979:63)

What this scenario may actually be demonstrating, however, is that the United States is being forced to join international economic institutions to compete in the global economy. It can be argued that the United States is not a lone hegemonic power in some hierarchical order, and in fact that a structural shift has taken place and has shaped the system in a way that has forced the unit-level actors to become competitive in other ways, namely through economic inter-dependency.

Institutions are often created for specific interests, or as Judith Goldstein and Robert Keohane discuss in *Ideas and Foreign Policy* (1993), policy may often stem from ideas that later become imbed-ded in institutions. Institutions are often created for one specific pur-pose, but that role changes over time and takes on a constraining power or purpose that is quite unrecognizable to those that envi-sioned it. In fact, such institutions may become unwieldy forces that are no longer tools of a nation or group but rather the master that wields the sword. G. John Ikenberry's (1993) study of the postwar economic settlement demonstrates that this concept may have oc-curred as economic policy was being forged according to the eco-nomic interests of well-placed elites who embraced Keynesianism rather than in the interests of any nation-state. I am quite certain that those individuals who sat down at Bretton Woods would have been quite surprised at the long-lasting effects the postwar settlement created, not only in the forces of capitalism, but from the effects of monetary policy and Westernization as well.

The system remains anarchic, and there are still units that affect, and are impacted by, the structure, all of which make up the system. It is plausible then that the definition of power may have changed from military to economic, but the fact remains that while some units seek to maximize power, others will merely seek enough power to slip comfortably into the structure.

The units may have also changed. Since medieval times, interna-tional relations theorists have been focusing on the nation-state as the main actor of the unit-level analysis, though the scope and definition of what a nation-state is has changed since then as well. In the twenty-first century, it may be less necessary to banish Waltz's balance-of-power theory as outdated and no longer useful than it will be to reshape what scholars of international relations view as unit-level actors. Perhaps some of the unit-level actors will remain sovereign nation-states, while other unit-level actors will take on the shape of regional trading blocs, corporations, or other international institutions. The important factor will most likely remain the economic interests of the state, trading bloc, or individuals whose ideas and interests are imbedded in the institution, not necessarily the political sovereignty of the state where these interests are housed. Finally, the issue of power will remain key as the unit-level actors scramble in an anarchic system for a certain seat within the international system.

Each unit's actions will most certainly differ somewhat from another's as each makes various decisions on how to find its place within the structure, but "since the variety of actors and the variations in their actions are not matched by the variety of outcomes, we know that systemic causes are in play" (Waltz, 1979:57). The balance-of-power theory that Kenneth Waltz promotes, then is still an effective theory in understanding international relations in the post-bipolar era and particularly when used as a tool for analyzing the way a systemic approach can be used to demonstrate "how a structure shapes and shoves the units of a system" (Keohane, 1986: 336). But it is time for international relations scholars, as well as economic and trade policy makers, to understand the important role that international institutions play in the global system.

CONCLUSION

Critics of this study will question the premise that economic power has really surpassed military power, and I will press the issue further promoting the idea that economics has been the driving force of military hegemonic tendencies long before the end of the post-bipolar era. Policy is created by well-situated elites in the highest circles of government who either have the power to push through specific policy choices or, more importantly, to decide what policy options even make it onto the agenda in the first place.

G. John Ikenberry argues that elites within the U.S. government decided on a shift in economic policy from a hemispheric bloc to an internationally integrated bloc because it was in the best interests of the United States. "In the two decades between the world wars, the internationally oriented sectors of the American economy had expanded considerably, increasing the nation's stake in a wider capitalist world order" (Ikenberry, 1993:63–64). Due to the positioning of the United States following World War II and the new strength of the dollar due to the transfer of most of the world's gold supply into the United States, the United States would now benefit from a multilateral open world economy, so it pushed the policy through, creating institutions at Bretton Woods to fulfill those purposes, and the United States is still benefitting from it today.

The Federal Reserve came into existence at the culmination of the rising power of the corporate elites in America. An institution was created that would serve the financial interests of the capitalists who had just successfully accomplished the corporate consolidation of America at the end of the nineteenth century and were now taking the next step to secure their positions and their standard-of-living levels. The Federal Reserve served as the institution that would centralize the savings of America for the benefit of financial investors. Policy would be created to ensure that the old competitive banking system (and the risks that went with it for the investors who depended on the liquidity of the banking system) would be regulated by the central bank. Federal Reserve policy is supposed to be carried out in order to best serve the interests of the United States, to calm the ebbs and flows of the normal economic cycles. It has largely been successful in this attempt and has kept the purchasing power of consumers strong as well by keeping inflation in check, though it appears the Fed has turned a blind eye to other sectors of the economy.

As international banking has come under increased scrutiny due to economic woes throughout Asia and Latin America, it is necessary and prudent to take another look at the assets that banks use to support the credit issued to borrowers. The practice of buying and selling assets, whether domestically or abroad, requires a medium of exchange regarded as highly credible. As the value of assets that back up the currency decreases, whether in real terms or through a general perception, currency values themselves will decrease accordingly or the exchange rate will fluctuate. In countries with central banking institutions, there is no real guarantee on investment of the currency except for confidence in the government's ability to back up the stocks or bonds it issues. In times of panic, investors must have faith that their investments are still convertible, or they may sell off their assets in large quantities, causing a massive world economic crisis.

Central banking seems to be an effective tool in modern trading societies due to the importance placed on liquidity. As the regulators of currency, and in the role of lenders of last resort, central banking institutions can provide confidence to international financiers, which is important during normal economic cycles. Central banks may be less effective under more volatile scenarios, as recent economic problems have called into question whether monetary economics is always capable of stimulating investment through a lowering of interest rates. If confidence levels cannot be restored, it may very well be true that an institutional solution does not exist under the current banking system. The validity of the regulating function that central banks have, and the definition of many of the financial instruments that are allowed under the asset side of banking ledgers, is questionable and should be reevaluated. This question of credit has grown increasingly important as finance capital has replaced other forms of security.

This study examines banking in the United States, from its rocky historical beginnings through the creation of the banker's bank, and on to the study of how the powerful institution with international influence, known as the Fed, creates policy that perpetuates trade deficits in the United States and affects the entire world economy with every policy change. I am certain that students of international relations will question the study of a domestic institution in an international institution thesis; however, it should be noted that not studying institutions with international influence simply because they are not ruled by a supranational body (therefore not meeting the technical definition of an international organization) is overlooking the core of what makes international politics really work. Not only is this study valid on its own accord because of the Federal Reserve's overarching influence into global affairs, but also because by studying such an institution, theoretical generalizations can be made about how domestic institutions constrain nation-state policy. Institutional constraint thus demonstrates how the international power structure is controlled less by nationalistic power interests than by institutional interest or elite interests acted out through an institutional policy forum.

Chapter 3

Banking on the Fed
for a Healthy Economy

INTRODUCTION

Banking functions have financed domestic and foreign investment and international trade since antiquity. However, since banking assets have grown increasingly dependent on the stock market, the values of banking assets are less stable, thus lending more volatility to an already unstable global economy. The Federal Reserve System was established to regulate the flow of money and credit in the economy and provide stability. Central banks are the lenders of last resort and can provide credit through a number of mechanisms when private lenders have stretched their lending capacities to the limits due to reserve requirements.

Banking functions, whether actually provided by a bank or not, are at the very core of the modern global trading system. It is essential, then, to understand how banks work in order to understand trade.

When gold was still used as a means to do commerce with other countries, ships of gold would cross the Atlantic to purchase and sell goods. Once the Federal Reserve was created, gold was often moved from one country's vault to another's, as can still be witnessed today in the gold vaults of the New York Federal Reserve Bank when foreign central banks buy and sell gold. This means of doing commerce was hardly as convenient as the electronic transactions that are performed today. Besides the problem of hauling gold around, which was no small task due to the inconvenience and danger involved, the value of gold was often difficult to observe, as it was common to shave gold coins or mix the gold with other metals of a lesser value. Thus bars and coins often did not truly represent the value they depicted.

Even during the early stages of international commerce, bankers were drawing up lines of credit for merchants to do business, yet with the advent of finance capital and electronic transactions, credit has grown in importance. Everyone from the Wall Street stockbroker buying on margin to the college student using his or her own charge card is buying on credit. Therefore, any thesis dealing with trade must discuss credit and other banking functions because trade is merely the formal handshake in the cycle of the overall transaction, whereas the banking functions that led up to the transaction are the complex machinery that made the whole operation functional; and they are even more important in this chapter as we study the institution where bankers go to do their banking.

This chapter outlines the importance of credit for modern trading societies. It demonstrates the unpredictability of modern banking, as banks' asset portfolios have the possibility of being devalued or overvalued because much of the value of the asset portfolios relies on the stock market.

Banking has been tied to investment since the advent of capitalism. In the United States, corporate consolidation needed the centralization of banking reserves in order to promote the corporate capitalists' interests in regard to economic stability while at the same time pooling the savings of the country into a financing machine that would support investment and ensure the standard-of-living levels for corporate elites. The Federal Reserve System was the institutionalization of these interests. The banking industry, particularly in the larger financial centers, thrived in this environment.

In a sluggish economy it is easy to call into question banking practices as corporate and personal bankruptcy filings reach record levels, but even in the late 1990s, when the technology boom created millionaires out of the twenty-something crowd and the bulls were raving about the strength of the economy, the health of banking was still being questioned. The overall health of the banking sector in the late 1990s and into the early part of the twenty-first century will be examined in this chapter, analyzing an *Economist* survey of international banking and contemplating recent bailouts of hed; e funds.

Finally, a look back at the savings and loan debacle in the 1980s will demonstrate how successful policy implementation, not a policy implementation blunder, led to a massive taxpayer bailout. Deregulation is what led to the savings and loan crisis and is what the international banking sector is campaigning for now. Is deregulation the answer for a purportedly ailing banking industry? This chapter will attempt to answer the question of why an institution would create policies that may help one sector over another, or possibly even over the interests of the nation. If, as this thesis proposes, trade deficits are governed by U.S. policy, which is constrained by Federal Reserve policy, then institutions can constrain, and not only inform or react to, national policy, as has sometimes been proffered in conventional wisdom.

BANKING FUNCTIONS

Mancur Olson wrote in his seminal work *The Logic of Collective Action* that there is a general perception that the state works for and on behalf of the national interest (Olson, 1995:98). Whether this is the case or not, there are certainly policy actors that influence, constrain, inform, or act on the behalf of the state. The domestic policy actors in the United States that this work studies are the institutionalized interests of business elites, particularly culminating in the banking and finance interests with the Federal Reserve. International actors that constrain nation-state policy are numerous, including trade blocs, the World Trade Organization (WTO), the International Monetary Fund (IMF), the United Nations, and multinational corporations, to name just a few. There are certainly many actors that can constrain the policies and actions of nation-states if military power is not viewed as preeminent.

This study examines how banking affects trade policy, but it is not incomprehensible, or improbable, that other institutions' policies are forcing the hand of other global actors, as the expansion of the European Union might constrain the North American Free Trade Agreement (NAFTA) to incorporate the members of Mercosur to try and counterbalance the size and possible further expansion of the EU's marketplace for privileged trade.

Central banking is not necessarily essential to the functioning of a trading society, as historical analyses of the U.S. banking system have proven, although it does serve as an important regulating and stabilizing mechanism in an otherwise highly volatile capitalistic world. The functions of banking have changed over time, especially since the shift from a gold standard to a floating exchange rate system. Banking functions do not necessarily have to be carried out by a bank, and in fact, these functions are being carried out by major corporations on a growing scale in the United States. This particular type of banking function lies outside the regulating controls of central banks; however, this study addresses mostly central banking issues since these are the institutions that countries use as lenders of last resort. One can certainly question the validity of the regulating function that central banks have, and thus question the definition of many of the financial instruments that are allowed under the asset side of banking ledgers. With the Federal Reserve's unlimited capacity to buy bonds, which is essentially the function of making money, the only controls it has are arguably those that it places on itself.

A single currency that is stabilized by a central bank and backed up by a nation-state's government increases the value of the currency because it has credibility which raises the confidence levels of investors. If someone wishes to engage in the practice of buying and selling assets, whether domestically or abroad, a medium of exchange that is regarded as highly credible is a necessity. As the value of the assets that back up the currency decreases, whether in real terms or through a general perception, currency values themselves will decrease accordingly or the exchange rate, which is the price of departing with one currency for another, will fluctuate.

The issue that is discussed in Livingston's study (1986) of the origins of the Federal Reserve System centers on the debate over whether credit should be given for secured loans only, or also for unsecured loans. Most bankers practiced some form of security on their loans, but what constituted an asset was also heavily debated. There were, however, many successful businessmen who made their money solely on loans given to them on trust.

Many of the most successful and prosperous financiers and business men of the country acknowledge that they owe their success to the timely assistance of some friendly banker, who, instead of demanding security or scrutinizing closely the security offered for loan, has shut his eyes to what he knew did not exist and has accepted for his sole security the trust and confidence he reposed in the man. (Livingston, 1986:171)[1]

However, in the early 1900s, corporate capitalists did not want this type of credit to remain legal. They feared that it encouraged speculation and would destabilize the economy. Bankers were increasingly lending funds that were invested in the stock market, and these investments were beginning to make up larger percentages of the reserve assets of banks. Corporate businessmen wanted some sort of stabilization factor to control seasonal volatility that this type of investment created.

One of the benefits of centralizing the nation's reserves would be that a central authority could require banks that caused the seasonal problems at crop harvest time to keep larger reserve ratios. Forcing these banks to keep larger reserve ratios would give the banks less money to loan on call in the money market. The loans that were made on call were then invested in the stock market. Because the loans were made on call, when the banks demanded their money back at harvest time, the investors were often forced to sell off the stocks to pay back the loans. These large stock sell-offs would send shock waves throughout the financial markets by decreasing stock prices and undermining asset values.

The reserve ratios were later institutionalized along with secured loans as standard operating procedures in the passage of the Federal Reserve Act in 1913. The debate over what could be considered banking assets had been decided, and the wealthy businessmen had prevailed.

Bray Hammond (1985), in his Pulitzer Prize–winning book *Banks and Politics in America: From the Revolution to the Civil War*, gives a long and detailed account of the debates that took place throughout the nineteenth century about what could be placed on the asset side of the ledger. Different banks had different practices throughout time since there was no Federal Reserve System. The assets, for example, were government and private loans, gold, accounts with other banks, commercial paper, and mortgages.

Agrarians in the United States often practiced their own form of banking. Often farmers in the South and West would trade on credit. Even goods bought in local stores would often be bought on credit, with the land and crops serving to secure the loan that would then be paid off at harvest time. Some deals were even done in a straight barter system, which was still a secured loan system.

Hammond's study is interesting in light of a world that has now readily accepted central banking as a necessary and positive regulator of the monetary supply. This function is the banking aspect that Hammond deems most crucial, even in today's Federal Reserve System. He claims that the National Bank Act, signed into law in 1864, required that

banks maintain reserves proportional to their liabilities . . . was all-important. It . . . [is] what good bankers had always observed, voluntarily. It made the pledge of securities a pretentious and cumbersome formality. A step of great evolutionary significance was taken, also in half-conscious, incidental fashion, by providing that required reserves might be partly in the form of bank credit. . . . The adoption of this arrangement . . . has led to the stage reached in the 20th century where the reserves of banks, as required by federal law, comprise no specie or other cash whatever, but exclusively amounts due from the Federal Reserve Banks. (Hammond, 1985:731–732)

While reserve banking is undoubtedly a necessary and crucial part of modern trade and commerce, it is considerably more debatable that the financial instruments modern banking utilizes are, in fact, secure, and whether or not they should fall under the asset portfolios of banks. The corporate elites of the era, however, felt that getting hold of the nation's savings and investing it in the stock markets was, in fact, furthering the national interest.

The system's major functions were to make available to particular industries the increasing savings of society as a whole and to manage periodic crises so as to maintain the existing distribution of income. As the pivot of a social system organized by the requirements of profitable commodity production, the banking apparatus had to be equal to the capacities of commodity production. In the late nineteenth and early twentieth centuries— then as now—this meant being equal to the capacities of the large corporations. . . . Interbank competition for reserves in the pursuit of short-term profit, for example, had to be stopped if "anarchy and chaos in times of stress" were not to destroy a price system under which the profitability of great investment in large fixed capital had become predictable. (Livingston, 1986:227)

As businesses or even entire countries become increasingly dependent on international trade, currency values become more important because the value will determine price levels. Friedrich List argued in the nineteenth century that price levels depend largely on the level of economic activity and the solvency of the banking system. Adam Smith had argued that price levels were neutral, but List countered Smith arguing that price levels are not neutral, especially under short-term fluctuations when long-term contracts have been signed. He writes that if

[price levels] fluctuate frequently and violently, disarrangements arise which throw the economy of every individual, as well as that of society, into confusion. Whoever has purchased raw materials at high prices, cannot under low prices, by the sale of his manufactured article, realise again that sum in precious metals which his raw materials have cost him. Whoever has bought at high prices landed property and has left a portion of the purchase money as a mortgage debt upon it, loses his ability of payment and his property; because, under diminished prices, probably the value of the entire property will scarcely equal the amount of the mortgage. Whoever has taken leases of property under a state of high prices, finds himself ruined by the decrease in prices, or at least unable to fulfil the covenants of his leases. The greater the rising and falling of prices, and the more frequently that fluctuations occur, the more ruinous is their effect on the economical conditions of the nation and especially on credit. (List, 1983: 275)

List's argument is especially relevant when discussing credit as it pertains to trade. List was making an argument for introducing tariffs that were later adopted and played a major role in the escalation of wealth and power of the United States. In *The Works of Alexander Hamilton* (1850), Hamilton made similar arguments about introducing tariffs to create asset-backed securities that the new nation's financial structure would be based upon, and while both men are largely remembered as advocates of protecting infant industries in a pre-industrialization era in U.S. history, one of their main reasons for advocating protectionism was to create financial assets through tariffs and to develop a banking system that could create liquidity. The theory advocated a system that would thrive on a banking industry supported by bonds in which the people would have confidence. The tariffs would provide the financial assets to found the system.

The Americans were almost wholly dependent on English manufactured goods throughout the period of the early nineteenth century, and due to a massive trade deficit, much of the nation's gold
supply was being shipped to England to pay off the debt. As the
banks sent their gold overseas, they had less to lend, and a credit
crisis arose.

These exports of bullion, however, as they undermine the American system
of paper circulation, necessarily lead to the ruin of the credit of the American banks, and therewith to general revolutions in the prices of landed
property and of the goods in circulation, and especially to those general
confusions of prices and credit which derange and overturn the economy
of the nation. . . . The destruction and convulsions of commerce and in
credit, as well as the reduction in consumption, are attended with disad-
vantages to the welfare and happiness of individuals and to public order,
from which one cannot very quickly recover and the frequent repetition of
which must necessarily leave permanently ruinous consequences. (List,
1983:274)

In an era when the gold standard is no longer used and commerce
occurs almost entirely through a system of credit, reserve banking
has increased in importance. A chronic trade deficit may result in a
shrinking money supply, or worse may cause an increase in the
money supply if investors abroad lose confidence in the currency
and send it back in large quantities. If a tightening of credit occurs
due to the perceived crisis, banks will begin to restrict their loans,
which fall under their asset portfolios, because they are required to
meet the liabilities on the accounts, thus requiring higher reserves.
Higher reserves means less money to lend, which theoretically means
less investment can take place.[2]
    Keynes advocated that a lack of confidence generally leads to less
consumption, which naturally induces a decrease in production,
thereby decreasing the incentive for future investment. This situation
can turn into a vicious downward spiral that may be difficult to
reverse. Under this type of scenario monetary economics could be
ineffective.

There is the possibility . . . that, after the rate of interest has fallen to a
certain level, liquidity-preference may become virtually absolute in the sense
that almost everyone prefers cash to holding a debt which yields so low a

rate of interest. In this event the monetary authority would have lost effective control over the rate of interest. (Keynes, 1964:207)

Although a large portion of the world's currency was backed by gold or other precious metals through much of the twentieth century,[3] credit has been documented as far back as the fourth century B.C. In Edward Cohen's study of Athenian banking he demonstrates that although buying and selling on credit was technically illegal in Athenian society, in practice the *trapezai* had a sophisticated banking system that financed commerce and maritime trade.

Where payments were made not by actual transfer of coins but by entry on the books of the bank favoring the recipient's account, the need for physical coins, "commodity money," was obviously eliminated. This appears to have happened so routinely that the Athenians even had a term (diagraphe) for the cashless settlements of debts through bank entries. To the extent that banks could anticipate handling payment orders and other calls by written memoranda (hypomnemata) and not by cash, the amount of currency reserves kept by the bankers might be reduced, with a corresponding increase in the money supply through additional bank lending or bank spending. (Cohen, 1997:17)

This question of credit has grown increasingly important as finance capital has replaced other forms of security. What the Athenians were practicing over 2,000 years ago was essentially what Alexander Hamilton was trying to promote in the United States in the late eighteenth and early nineteenth centuries. Countries like the United States and Germany that were lacking assets, primarily gold, to back up their currencies needed to create currencies that were perceived to be as good as gold.[4] The United States never accepted this notion completely until 1973, when the gold standard was converted to a floating exchange rate system.

As banks now rely on the stock market, it seems that markets are increasingly more volatile, despite central banking institutional attempts at regulating such distress on the world's economies. As Keynes (1964) pointed out in *The General Theory of Employment, Interest, and Money*, it is investment, and the climate that leads to it, that creates the assets used by the banking system. Financial instruments now make up large portions of the asset portfolios that banks rely on.

J. Lawrence Broz (1997) in *The International Origins of the Federal Reserve System* concludes that central banks provide the lender of last resort that makes this modern system feasible, whereby investors get the liquid assets they need by selling their stocks and bonds in times of crisis. In the United States, as in other countries with central banking institutions, there is no asset security, or guarantee on investment of the currency, except for confidence in the federal government and its ability to back up the bonds, with U.S. dollars as their receipts. Convertibility of assets, or the perceived ability to convert assets to cash, such as what bankers call "near money," is one of the most important policy tools used to keep investors from selling off their assets in large quantities, causing a massive world economic crisis. Broz states that:

No matter how broad and deep financial markets are, there are times at which they become illiquid. A primary function of central banks is to provide liquidity to the market during such periods. This last mechanism is crucial, since it implies that a high degree of certainty as to the value of a nation's currency and articulated domestic markets in internationally accessible financial instruments are not enough. (Broz, 1997:63)

Central banks have the responsibility of not only keeping currency values at an acceptable level, but also of ensuring that the creation of money also keeps the international balance of payments in check so as not to create panic in the perceived value of the national currency, leading to massive disinvestment or asset sell-offs.

Or, on the other hand, it may also be true that corporations will soon "create" so much of the money used in commerce that a central bank's power will be severely hobbled as its regulatory functions do not control this type of transaction anyway. It would seem prudent that under this scenario, which is largely underway, an international regulatory institution should be created to oversee and control unwieldy global economic upheavals.

A LOOK AT THE HEALTH OF MODERN BANKING

Banking policy has, over time, installed mechanisms, such as the centralization of reserves and the diversification of loans over many different states, to avoid local economic crises. However, international investments into emerging economies and riskier loans have proved less manageable and more volatile. What will the future of banking look like? The end of the twentieth century saw just as much volatility, or perhaps more, than the beginning. The twenty-first century does not appear to be starting off much differently, and supposedly banks are much better at risk management now that they have complex models with sophisticated tracking programs to calculate risk ratios.

Banks have grown increasingly dependent on the stock market to bolster asset portfolios, and the stockholders of banks have been putting pressure on banks to increase their own stock prices. Banks have tried to cut costs through such means as mergers, leading to the reconsolidation of the industry, and have had to get involved in riskier investments to try to make more money.

In the April 17, 1999 issue of *The Economist*, a survey of international banking was reported entitled, "On a Wing and a Prayer." *The Economist*'s assessment of the banking sector was that it was, at best, in trouble and in need of reform, and that, at worst, it could cause a major global recession. The assessment would probably still hold true today, and it could be due to the management practices of corporations that the banking industry is at risk. Ironically, it is the same segment of society whose predecessors gave rise and status to the banking industry that now could be causing its collapse. The story behind the rise of the banking industry which culminated in the establishment of the Federal Reserve System will be told in a later chapter, but suffice it to say for now that the capitalists who came to banks looking for credit in early times are now shopping around, and they are finding that the best deals are not usually with banks, particularly in the United States. "Only about 30% of America's financing needs come from banks and 70% from the markets" (Cookson, April 17, 1999:17–18).

Why have investors started shopping for credit elsewhere? The reason is that the credit ratings of banks have demonstrated that the industry is not very healthy. The debt crisis that occurred in the early 1980s, mostly in Latin America, was largely blamed on the banking industry's lack of vigilance in risk management and failure to keep proper capital to risk asset ratios on their loan portfolios. "In 1988, a committee of international bankers . . . came to a landmark agreement: it decreed that, by 1992, internationally active banks should have capital equal to 8% of their risk assets" (Cookson, April 17, 1999:8). The agreement has become known as the Basle Accord.

The Basle Accord, with all of its good intentions, has had some unexpected effects in the financial world, not the least of which is pricing banks out of the market in the competition with other lenders for the best borrowers. Therefore, while the Basle Accord attempted to regulate risk and stabilize the international economy, it has actually caused banks to search for less-than-stellar borrowers; hardly the risk-reducing behavior the Basle Accord was looking to achieve.

At the moment, there are three classes of borrower: those for which banks need to put aside the full 8% capital; those for which they need only a fifth of that; and those for which they need none at all. . . . Into the first category go all non-financial companies, whatever their credit worthiness. . . . Mutual funds, for example, have no capital requirements, so in theory they can lend much more cheaply. This is one reason, say bankers, why they have been priced out of the market for better-quality borrowers. If the capital requirements of lending to Microsoft, say, were reduced to reflect the quality of its credit, the banks would be more competitive with the capital markets.
   The incentives in the second and third categories are still more perverse. Lending to banks in OECD countries, or to the countries themselves, requires only a fraction of the 8%, or nothing at all, to be put aside. . . . So, lending to a South Korean bank requires only one-fifth of the amount of capital needed for lending to General Electric. (Cookson, April 17, 1999: 9)

The Basle Accord is under fire from the banking industry and may see some badly needed reform. Change will have to come amid a sea of political strife, however, as Germany and Japan in particular will seek exemptions and compromise in key areas such as commercial and landesbank lending.
   Lending to high-risk borrowers poses great risks to banks and the economy in general. Because consumers are borrowing and buying more on credit, a larger percentage of their paychecks is going toward paying those debts.
   When economic slowdowns occur, and they always do, unemployment rates rise and loan defaults become more frequent. As more and more banks' debts go bad, banks will suffer, some will go under, and stock values will decrease, possibly sending the economy spiraling into a recession.
   1998 was a year that sparked international concern over the econ-

omy as emerging markets around the world were on the verge of collapse. The so-called "Asian Flu" led to an upheaval in financial markets across the globe as currency devaluations and collapsing banks caused a credit crisis that not even Federal Reserve interest rate cuts could completely dissolve. That same year the Federal Reserve had to calm international markets with the infamous hedge fund bailout, which still could not completely avert a credit crunch or calm investors' fears. In 2001 the Federal Reserve cut the federal funds rate to its lowest level in decades, but the rate cuts could do very little to bolster collapsing consumer confidence. This reality directs questions at the very heart of modern monetary economic theory and should make investors, theoreticians, academics, and policy makers alike ask whether an institutional mechanism to control investment panic actually exists, even after the consolidation of the savings of America was successfully accomplished with the creation of the Federal Reserve System.

The bailout of Long-Term Capital Management (LTCM), one of the industry's most prestigious hedge funds, led analysts to take another look at the security of bank assets. It seems logical that an internationally acclaimed hedge fund boasting among its board members "a former vice-chairman of the Federal Reserve, one of Wall Street's most revered traders, and a couple of Nobel-prize–winning economists" (Cookson, April 17, 1999:3) would be a pretty good credit risk to any bank, let alone some of the world's largest and most capital-intensive. However, when LTCM invested in Russian bonds and then the bonds lost half of their value, LTCM was forced to liquidate assets across the globe to pay for their losses. Measuring market risk in modern financial markets is not a science, as the recent crisis demonstrated, even though investment firms and banks alike would like to make their customers believe otherwise. Riskier debt is being issued by banks to such funds in order to keep their own margins at acceptable levels, but "hedge funds such as Long-Term Capital Management, whose demise was averted only by a bailout coordinated by the Federal Reserve, proved a lot less secure than they had thought" (Cookson, April 17, 1999:7).

Are banks being squeezed due to unfair regulations and prohibitive reserve requirements? Many banking policy experts are calling for a deregulation of the industry so that banks can compete for better customers and lend out larger portions of their asset portfolios. American banks continually received lower credit ratings throughout the 1990s and into the early 2000s, making them less healthy now than even two decades ago. The ratings are down because the risk of default is high. The equation is as simple as that.

Though deregulation is often the quick fix key in monetary policy circles and in financial markets in general, a quick trip down memory lane can demonstrate a situation where policy implementation worked too well. The savings and loan debacle in the United States is an example. The Fed, through persuasion and policy constraint on Congress, was involved in a deregulation measure that catered to the industry's interests, and definitely not the nation's interest. It demonstrates that deregulation may only be a quick fix, not a solution for the long-term benefit of the industry or the nation.

BANKING POLICY IMPLEMENTATION AND THE SAVINGS AND LOAN DEBACLE

(The following excerpt is adapted from Michael Robinson's book, *Overdrawn: The Bailout of American Savings*.)

Ed Gray, the Chairman of the Federal Home Loan Bank Board, the top regulatory body for the savings and loan industry, was driving down a French highway on the morning of Tuesday, August 21, 1984. He had been summoned back to the Federal Reserve from his European vacation to meet with Paul Volcker and to deal with an unfolding catastrophe. American Savings and Loan Association of Stockton, California, the nation's largest thrift, with more than $30 billion in assets, had experienced a tidal wave of withdrawals for the past few weeks where depositors were removing hundreds of millions of dollars each day.

Gray was convinced that the collapse of American would bankrupt the Federal Savings and Loan Insurance Corporation (FSLIC), the industry's insurance fund. . . . He had been expecting trouble for months. American was by far the largest thrift in the country, but it was not the only one with severe problems. The whole industry was headed for disaster. . . .

Once known for their conservative business practices, S&Ls now gambled federally insured funds on a wide array of risky investments. Unless these investments were curbed, the industry might decline to the point that a taxpayer bailout would be needed to rescue hundreds of S&Ls, a solution Gray strongly opposed. . . . It was a gross oversimplification, but in a word, the trouble was *deregulation*. (Robinson, 1990:1–2)

This was the beginning of the unraveling of the savings and loan debacle. Those like Gray who had endorsed deregulation were thrilled with the unprecedented powers that Congress and state legislatures across the nation had bestowed on the thrifts. Now, however, even those who were the most stalwart in championing deregulation were blaming the collapse of the savings and loan industry on the irresponsible system.

Is deregulation the causal force behind the savings and loan debacle? This section will take the reader through a brief history of events in the savings and loan industry prior to the policy decision to deregulate it. It will then move on to argue the pros and cons of deregulation of such an industry and will conclude with the policies that should have been implemented in this situation, as well as in future dealings with other government-backed industries like the savings and loan industry.

History

The housing market in the United States has followed a cyclical pattern. Construction was on the rise at the outset of the twentieth century after following a slight decline in the late nineteenth century. World War I proved to be a governor, but housing production was again on the rise immediately after the war, reaching its climax in 1925. From 1925 through World War II, construction was down considerably. Immediately following World War II, America experienced a housing (and baby) boom. The money that was available for housing was directly linked to the Keynesian policies that the federal government implemented shortly following the war. Along with federal deposit insurance, the government placed regulations on banks and savings and loan institutions, also known as "thrifts," that limited the interest rates that banks could pay on time deposits, allowing thrifts to win bids for savings deposits, while requiring them to invest nearly all of their funds in home loans in exchange for favorable income tax benefits. By 1965, only twenty years after the end of World War II, the assets of thrifts had grown from $8.7 billion in 1945, to $110.4 billion (Eichler, 1989:18–21).

In 1966 the party was beginning to fade. The housing market fell to a postwar low. Residential construction had quickly outpaced the consumer demand for such housing. Economic growth, population growth, and productivity were all down. Interest rates rose as the Federal Reserve tried to curb inflation, so depositors looked to commercial banks and Treasury bills as alternative investment sources while savings and loans grew desperate as their assets were being depleted by a tidal wave of withdrawals.

President Johnson refused to inhibit spending, and in fact chose to boost federal spending levels and increase the money supply by the Federal Reserve to pay for it. Inflation rates soared twice more after 1966, in 1970 and then again in 1975. The 1980s brought a new administration and with it a new policy in dealing with the savings and loan industry: deregulation (Eichler, 1989:24–32).

Deregulation was aimed at conquering inflation and possibly keeping the FSLIC from bailing out the industry. Escaping the bail-out would be achieved by allowing the industry to compete with commercial banks by making risky investments, far out of their original realm of home mortgages. The outcome was obviously not as anyone had hoped as the bailout skyrocketed far beyond even the most pessimistic economists' projections and resulted ultimately in the demise of the FSLIC.

Pro-Deregulation

There is a paradigm that supports the deregulation of the savings and loan industry. Deregulation actually began during the Carter administration with the airline and trucking industries. Liberals and conservatives alike joined the deregulation bandwagon as inflation continued to rise dramatically through the late 1970s. As inflation soared, interest rates grew with it, and savings and loans were forced to pay interest rates of 8 to 10 percent while only receiving 4 to 6 percent on their thirty-year home mortgages, which had been negotiated before the years of inflation (Krugman, 1995:161).

An analysis conducted at the Salomon Brothers Center for the Study of Financial Institutions by Professor George J. Benston points out that the Keynesian policies in the inflationary years of the 1960s and 1970s were at the core of the savings and loan debacle.

Data indicates that savings and loan failures, on the average, appear primarily due to interest payments that exceeded interest income. Foreclosed mortgages played a small role. Brokered deposits may have played a role, although the relationship is not consistent. Very high rates of growth are associated with the failure of some savings and loans. Deregulated assets, though, do not appear responsible for failures. Nonmortgage commercial loans and consumer loans are not related to the failure. Nor are the two variables that are the subjects of special regulations—direct investments and growth—related to failure, on the average, although very high rates of growth appear to be important factors in the failure of several savings and loans. (Benston, 1986:73)

The study then went on to state that in fact some of the regulations that were left imposed were actually counterproductive.

The study does not indicate that deregulation of investment powers was a cause of the official failures. Consumer and commercial loans were negligible at the savings and loans that failed. Direct investments—defined as real estate held for development, investment, and resale, and equity investments in service corporation subsidiaries—were found to be neither a cause of failures nor responsible for higher FSLIC payouts at the associations that failed. On the contrary, the data . . . indicates that direct investments provided savings and loans with much higher earnings than did other operations, while reducing somewhat the variance of earnings. More meaningful than the variance as a measure of risk to the FSLIC is the extent to which earnings are negative. The study found an inverse relationship between negative total net earnings and the proportion of assets in direct investments. Hence, the regulation . . . that restricts direct investments to a maximum of ten percent of assets (unless the FSLIC-insured association obtains specific permission) appears to be counter-productive. (Benston, 1986:171–173)

There are those who champion the protection of deposit insurance funds, who still feel that restraints needed to be removed from savings and loans. In a Brookings Institution study, the task force stated, "In the interest of improving the efficiency, quality, and range of financial services offered the public, depository institutions and affiliated firms should be subject to fewer constraints" (Brookings Task Force, 1989:viii). This study was later used as the format to implement the deregulation policies.

The study points out that regulations in fact may have been the reason for the debacle. The study concludes that although competitors of the savings and loan institutions were allowed to invest and engage in a variety of banking activities, such as "taking in insured deposits and extending commercial and consumer loans by exploiting various legal devices" (Brookings Task Force, 1989:viii), the savings and loans themselves were heavily restricted in these areas. Hence they failed to obtain permission to expand into other nonbank activities even though many of those activities were not risky ventures and, in fact, could have helped buffer other risks assumed by these institutions. The task force, which was put together to restructure or reform the depository institutions, claimed that these same restrictions imposed "serious costs" to the depositors and the institutions themselves by not allowing the savings and loans to achieve full economies of scale and scope in the financial market (Brookings Task Force, 1989:4). These findings were in line with the *Radcliffe Report on Monetary Policy*, which stated:

Any severely restrictive control of these (lenders) is certain, over a period of time, to be defeated by the development of rival institutions; during the interim, the community will have suffered loss by interference with the most efficient channels of lending. (Kaldor, 1982:10)

Anti-Deregulation

Now we must give voice to the school of thought that believed that the deregulation of the industry was completely at the heart of the savings and loan scandal. The mood of the general populace was definitely swinging in favor of deregulation when these measures were enacted. So many policy scholars have admitted that it is far easier to envision policy error with the advantage of 20–20 hindsight. In Robert Lane's "Market Justice, Political Justice," he asks, "What am I willing to give up for the policies and services desired? . . . The grocer, made unhappy by the taxes he pays to support welfare, is happy to receive the custom of his welfare clients" (Lane, 1986:400). Just as in this scenario, the taxpayers who were unhappy about footing the bill of the savings and loan crisis were certainly thrilled at the low mortgage rates and high interest rates on deposits they were able to receive during the 1980s.

The precursor to the deregulation of the industry is one of the few realities upon which opposing ideologies can concur: inflation. During the 1970s inflation soared while the income and assets of the savings and loans consisted mainly of meager thirty-year mortgages bringing in 4 to 6 percent. The savings and loans were being forced to pay out double that just to stay competitive with banks.

In response to the soaring inflation, the Federal Reserve opted to tighten the money supply, which ultimately shot the economy into a recession. Deregulation had begun before the recession, however, which doomed its opportunity for success almost before it even began.

Initiating deregulation during an interest rate crisis almost guaranteed that deregulation would fail because Congress could not undo overnight the damage that . . . had been building in the thrifts for decades. In particular, Congress could not lawfully rewrite the fixed-rate mortgages of thrifts. These mortgages were at the heart of the industry's reported [losses] . . . Instead, Congress granted thrifts powers to make loans and investments that supposedly would be more profitable and thus enable the thrifts to generate earnings to offset the losses incurred in funding low-interest-rate mortgages with high-cost deposits. (Hearing before the Committee on the Budget, 1989:190–191)

This freedom to make loans and investments opened up a whole new can of worms. Unwise ventures by a new breed of investors quickly flooded the market, and why not? It was a win-win situation, or so it seemed. High-risk investments could make some people very rich, while losses were insured by the FSLIC. It was basically a license to gamble without running the risk of losing any of your own money.

The two pieces of legislation that were primarily responsible for eliminating the governmental controls and the system of interest rate ceilings were the Depository Institutions Deregulation and Monetary Control Act of 1980, which became law on March 31, 1980, Public Law 96–221, and was sponsored by Representative St. Germain in the 96th Congress; and the Garn–St.Germain Depository Institutions Act of 1982, which became law on October 15, 1982 as Public Law 97–320, and was sponsored again by Representative St. Germain in the 97th Congress. The latter piece of legislation served as an amendment to the former. These two acts, respectively, promised to eliminate controls and allow further, significant flexibility in liability management, (Balderston, 1985:16). As official language in the debate over a proposed amendment to the policy stated,

[It] would remove this competitive inequity and effectuate the objective of the Garn–St. Germain bill. . . . If banks are to have a good reason to do what is their proper function in our country—namely, be aggressive in seeking deposits and be prudent in making commercial loans with those deposits—they need incentives and a chance to compete. (98th Congress, 2nd Session Vote, 1984)

Implementation of the new policy included an inducement strategy. Congress had cleared the way for thrifts to make commercial loans and investments while removing the interest rate ceilings and reserve requirements that were imposed on them, with few oversight mechanisms or regulations, or none at all. The savings and loans were given discretionary power to oversee their own asset portfolios. This scenario created a playground for speculators as the credit industry became a buyer's market. Congress figured that with these new inducements investors and bankers alike would naturally have an incentive to make more money, which would in turn save Congress from bailing out the industry and having to deal with any related political fallout. The policy authorized the Federal Home Loan Bank Board, the top regulatory body for the savings and loan industry, to permit the Federal Savings and Loan Insurance Corporation (FSLIC) "to provide assistance to insured institutions when severe financial conditions exist which threaten the stability of a significant number of insured institutions. [This] includes deposits in the institution or the purchase of securities as a type of assistance" (*Garn–St. Germain*, 1982). Possibly even more important to the solvency of the system was that requirements were also waived that a portion of net earnings of banks be set aside in a reserve account, as was previously necessary.

The liberation of lenders also meant liberation of borrowers from the chains of government regulations. The market would now decide what rates would be paid for credit and other banking services for the first time since the New Deal had been enacted. This freedom was monumental, especially in dealing with interest rate ceilings that lending institutions could charge because such ceilings had previously been heavily regulated in accordance with the Keynesian paradigm that easily obtained credit was the necessary catalyst in stimulating economic growth. Such deregulation was, at the very least, precarious in that the domestic economy was borrowing at its highest level since World War II, and doing it at the highest real interest rates of the twentieth century (Greider, 1989:8).

Savings and loans were lending astronomical amounts of money to finance high-risk endeavors, and sometimes many such loans were given to one borrower, further jeopardizing profitable returns. A blatant example of these types of investments occurred at the now infamous Silverado Savings and Loan.

An astonishing sixty-six percent of Silverado's loan portfolio was concentrated in high-risk loans. More than twenty-two percent of its loans were already bad . . . forcing the thrift to recognize $40 million in loan losses [in 1985 alone]. (Wilmsen, 1991:95–96)

This combination of the recession and the principal-agent problem, along with improper oversight of the implementation process, ultimately led to the demise of the policy. If the government had been prepared to swallow the losses of the savings and loans in 1980, it would have shut them down and paid approximately $15 billion in federal money; but by deregulating in hopes for quick returns on high-risk investments, that figure skyrocketed to over $166 billion in 1989. Nearly all of the money was lost specifically to bad, high-risk investments. The General Accounting Office claims that the thrift scandal is still placing tax burdens on U.S. citizens but that the ultimate cost of the bailout is truly unknown. A number of analysts have claimed that the bailout cost the nation nearly $1 trillion in the end.

All across the country, savings and loans became financiers of speculative developments, projects that could conceivably make a lot of money, but were more likely to lose it. . . . If the economy had boomed through the whole decade, if oil prices had (remained) high, if real interest rates had not risen so much, it is just possible that this game of "double or nothing" (deregulation), might have worked. But, instead, oil prices collapsed and the economy passed through a major recession. (Krugman, 1995:162)

Several years of inflation left the savings and loan industry incapable of competing with the banking industry because of the burden of earlier low-interest home mortgages. Deregulation in the early 1980s exposed the FSLIC to deposit insurance claims due to poor investment decisions by thrifts and led to the eventual bankruptcy and demise of that institution (Kormendi, 1989:19). Like many policies, the plan worked on paper. However, when the actual implementation came, although the policy's inducements did create the incentives to borrow and invest that Congress had hoped for, the outcome was clearly not what the proponents of the policy had envisioned.

First and foremost, the principal-agent problem existed. Congress, hoping to avoid paying an estimated $15 billion in federal money and the political fallout that such a bailout would cause, wanted to deregulate the industry in hopes that it could pull itself out of financial distress. The Federal Home Loan Bank Board wanted desperately to catch up and compete with the private banking industry, and thus allowed high-risk investments with the hope of high payoffs. However, there was a whole new breed of investors that cared nothing about the goals of Congress or the Federal Home Loan Bank Board, and these were the agents, in the principal-agent scenario, that Congress was depending upon to save the industry. While it was true that the investors wanted to make a great deal of money, which may indeed have pulled the industry out of distress as Congress intended, the motives of the principal and the agents varied greatly.

Deregulation was not the only factor in the savings and loan scandal; however, it compounded the severity of the pain. Deregulation policies allowed for excessive growth in FSLIC liabilities and gave the green light for irresponsible investments. Controls should have been left on the savings and loan industry to more closely monitor the situation. Policy makers wanted to remove restrictions to allow more flexible investment, and that probably should have been done long ago. However, controls that monitored how much of the industry's assets were being invested, and at what rate, should have been more closely monitored.

Similar problems could occur with the deregulation of international banks, forcing the Federal Reserve to bail out bad gambles in order to save the world from an economic meltdown, as the they had to do with LTCM in 1998.

Regulation is not the answer to every problem, and certainly it can often be at the very root of the problem, as later sections that deal with policy making and accountability will demonstrate. However, if governments are going to continue to guarantee the solvency of non-governmental or quasi-governmental institutions in the future, then we must learn from our mistakes in the savings and loan crisis and institute tighter controls. As Senator Kohl stated at the Hearing before the Subcommittee on Government Information and Regulation in regard to regulating GSEs (Government-Sponsored Enterprises):

We have already learned through the S&L crisis that . . . loose regulation coupled with a Federal guarantee is a recipe for disaster, and this Nation simply cannot afford another massive taxpayer bailout. (Hearing before the Subcommittee on Government Information and Regulation, 1991)

RELATING MODERN BANKING PROBLEMS TO THE SAVINGS AND LOAN CRISIS

The savings and loan debacle stemmed from numerous factors, but from a policy implementation standpoint, the deregulation policy induced speculative capitalists to take out loans and invest. Deregulation was a policy move that proved to be risky and ill-advised. This was a policy that was created because the policy makers refused to tackle the powerful banking industry, knowing that the political repercussions from battling an industry that could finance an army of lobbyists and marketing techniques could prove to be politically fatal. The result was a massive taxpayer bailout of an industry. Although the bailout of the savings and loan industry was costly, there is another scenario which is even more frightening, and it could hit when we least expect it.

The other scenario lies on the other end of the "feel good" spectrum. It seems that with a booming economy, as in the latter half of the 1990s in the United States, lenders are more lackadaisical in checking the creditworthiness of borrowers. The credit industry soared to new heights during this time period as everyone from the phone companies and car manufacturers to the traditional credit card companies and banks sought the future savings of consumers, and Americans were buying on credit like never before.

But in business, as the supply grows larger, the profit margins begin to dwindle. The situation can be seen in an example of a satellite television dealer who set up shop in the mid-1980s in Salt Lake City, Utah. Originally there were only a handful of dealers west of the Mississippi River, so the dealer in Salt Lake City was installing satellite dishes in California, Idaho, Wyoming, Arizona, and Nevada and was making a profit margin of nearly 300 percent due to the demand for the product and the exclusivity of his dealership. As more and more consumers became aware of an alternative to cable television and the demand grew larger, naturally more satellite dealerships began opening throughout the United States. Now, an interested consumer can flip through the phone book and find numerous pages of stores or dealerships in Salt Lake City alone that sell and install satellite television systems. The same dealer who was making 300 percent profit margins is now selling just above his cost, and is selling from a room in his house because profit margins will not allow him to maintain a showroom.

Economists will argue that eventually enough satellite dealers will go out of business, or redirect their business elsewhere, so that the industry will come back into a healthy balance. The realignment should theoretically cause the supply and demand curves to meet at a price that is appealing to the consumer yet allows a profit margin large enough to support the dealers who have remained in business.

In times when the credit industry is eager to give out loans, like the late 1990s, lenders will dish out loans to practically anyone who will take one. Even in a sluggish economy, some businesses are so eager to get consumers to spend that they will issue credit to everyone from heavily indebted college students (with no assets or steady income except subsidized, or even unsubsidized, student loans) to entrepreneurs who just filed for bankruptcy. Nearly anyone can get a credit card, a gas card, a department store card, and a phone card, to name just a few. The good news for consumers is that, at least in the short term, interest rates have steadily declined. As banks and other credit issuing companies compete for consumers, they have had to offer cheaper mortgages and car loans while giving incentives to the saving class to deposit their money into savings accounts or mutual funds so as to shore up asset portfolios, creating more lending ability. However, this creates more liabilities to those who deposit their money, and with low interest rates leaves little incentive to invest. If banks offer higher interest rates on savings or other time deposits, they are increasing their liabilities further and must balance their portfolios by increasing their assets, loans.

Unfortunately, as the market gets more and more competitive and the race to issue credit becomes tighter, the market becomes saturated at some point and banks are forced to go after less creditworthy investors. Unfortunately, these assets may be liabilities in themselves.

Banks, or any companies that engage in banking activity, depend on loans to make a profit. Like the satellite dealer selling dishes to make a profit, banks are essentially selling money to make money. It is all a system of IOUs. The money that is put into the bank is owed to the depositor. Mortgages, car loans, and student loans are IOUs to the bank. Banks go out of business when they can no longer meet their financial liabilities and thus are forced to liquidate their assets. They generally do this by selling the assets, the portfolio of IOUs, to another financial institution; then they settle their accounts.

Banks can get into trouble on both sides of the balance sheet. Just as the satellite dealer was forced to drop prices in line with the other dealers, bankers may be forced to drop interest rates on loans in line with the competition. Furthermore, as banks compete for customers with less than stellar credit, they will certainly see the rates of default increase, thus diminishing their assets. This is not unlike someone walking into the satellite dealer's store at night and walking off with a system without paying. A default on a loan, or any bad debt that needs to be written off, is basically a shoplifted asset. Sooner or later, if shopkeepers, or bankers, get shoplifted too much, they are going to go out of business.

CONCLUSION

Heavy lending, which relies on the stock market for its assets as most modern banking does, has the possibility of creating a massive credit crisis if and when there is a stock market correction that causes share prices to drop to historical averages. When share prices drop, asset values decline, leaving asset to liability ratios out of sync. Under this type of scenario banks would be forced to liquidate their assets and restrict further issuance of credit to pay off liabilities. If lending is restricted, many consumers will likely find it more beneficial to hold on to their cash rather than invest it in savings and time deposits, especially because banks may lower the interest they pay on such accounts to lower their liabilities. Therefore, as less money comes in to lend, there is less credit available for commerce and consumption. Less consumption causes manufacturers to slow down production to meet the slowing demand resulting in higher unemployment. A slowdown in production creates less incentive for investment, especially since credit is more costly and investors are less likely to borrow in order to invest, and thus the economy is driven into a downward spiral.

The Federal Reserve was created to suspend such a crisis and did avert a global meltdown by bailing out LTCM in the late 1990s, but has it created policy that will prevent a long-term slowdown in the U.S. economy? It seems likely that the Fed is only willing to intervene when either a global meltdown is imminent or consumer prices are inflating. It may be true that the Fed has created a gambling policy not unlike the policy used in deregulating the savings and loan industry.

This chapter has demonstrated the significance of banking, and more importantly credit, in global trade and commerce. From antiquity to the advent of capitalism, through the era of imperialism and industrialization, and finally into the age of technology, finance capital, and electronic commerce, someone engaging in banking functions has been behind the scenes making it all possible.

In the United States, industrialization and corporate consolidation created a new class of wealth and power, and the self-regulated banking system was considered a threat to the economic stability of the markets and the financial stability of investors. The creation of the Federal Reserve System was the institutionalization of this class' interests by regulating the economic ebbs through controlling the nation's money and credit. James Livingston noted that the corporate capitalists of the time knew what they were doing and had a specific strategy in mind. These events did not take place out of some natural progression as is often claimed in liberal economics. "These men were, of course, committed to remaking capitalism in the United States. The central banking apparatus we know as the Federal Reserve System is a monument to their commitment" (Livingston, 1986:228). Not only did the centralization limit the sporadic spurts of investment and market sell-offs at crop harvest time, but it pooled the savings of the middle class, creating more credit and power for the investing class.

Regulation of the banking sector is not necessarily a bad thing, particularly in the environment that has been created and accepted in the modern financial world. However, regulation should not be wielded merely to ensure the living standard of one class of people. Instead, government regulation should work toward the goal of raising the standard of living of the entire population. Deregulation in the past, as witnessed in the savings and loan debacle, has led to a lack of transparency, provided inducements for financial irresponsibility, and created incentives to gamble on risky investments. The prescription for the ailing banking industry is not deregulation, but quite possibly more regulation.

The Federal Reserve can be an agent of the national government and work on behalf of the national interest. It has the capability to create monetary policy, such as using reserve requirements and interest-rate management practices in a way that promotes the long-term economic health and international power status of the entire nation. Trade is a very important part of the health of the U.S. economy, and history has shown that nations, including the United States, have gone to war to open up markets. The Federal Reserve, as we shall see in the next chapter, has the power to create a balance of trade but has chosen to ignore trade deficits in favor of a strict anti-inflation policy and a strong dollar, both of which, at times, have exacerbated the trade deficit.

The Federal Reserve needs to reevaluate the health of the banking sector and further regulate the financial instruments that serve as assets in a way that promotes a healthy economy and raises the standard-of-living level for the entire nation. The Fed has the ability and the global attention to serve as a model for international organizations, demonstrating how an institution works in a cooperative and positive manner, thus providing long-term benefits to all of the parties involved, not just short-term gains for the financial and well-placed elite.

Chapter 4

The Cultural Evolution of Institutions in the United States

INTRODUCTION

This chapter focuses on the emergence of the Federal Reserve System as an institution and compares its emergence to the creation of the federal republic as two major instances when the ideas and interests of a specific group were imbedded into institutions in the United States. The two historical accounts demonstrate how ideas, groups, and institutions have made an impact on one of the most powerful nation-states in the international system. This chapter demonstrates how the neorealist model fails to recognize the importance of institutions in creating policy, and identifies and analyzes different types of power and how that power is used in the agenda-setting and policymaking process.

It is important to step back and look at the larger picture from time to time so as to recapture the intent of this analysis. As Chapters 3, 4, and 5 delve into the banking history and policies of the United States, it is easy to lose sight of the fact that this study is about the international system, not just U.S. banking and how it affects the U.S. trade deficit. In Chapter 2 it was stated that central banking policy directly affects whether or not a country has a trade deficit, and so it was important to understand why a central bank would or would not pursue a policy agenda that tried to achieve a trade balance. In a straight international economic or U.S. historical case study of the Federal Reserve System and its policies, it would be important to take specific policies and follow them through to implementation as a data-gathering technique for obtaining evidence. However, it is important to note here that this study is not using a case study as such a technique, which would prove deductive and less useful to the field of international relations. Rather, the research design is a case study itself, intended to look at the historical sequence of events and trade data in a study that proposes to demonstrate how the theory discovered in one macroeconomic system is generalizable to the whole or a part of the larger international system. Such a model requires looking at one system, in this case the U.S. banking system, and understanding how the conclusions are applicable to the larger international community.

The methodological distinction between using the case study as a data-gathering technique versus using the case study as the actual research design, or model around which the whole analysis takes place, is significant. On the one hand, the case study as a data-gathering technique intends to use the case study as evidence to demonstrate how the results of the case study itself are generalizable to the whole. On the other hand, the case study as a research design intends to demonstrate how the theory, not the results, are generalizable to the larger system.

Many balance-of-power systems theorists will argue that a study such as this should not even be undertaken because economic institutions, like regimes, are inconsequential when looking at the larger picture of the national interest. Waltz argues that states attempt to gain as much power as needed to fit into a comfortable position within the international structure, so that the states can then achieve other types of prosperity, such as economic affluence. The power is primarily military, not economic. This theory, which gave Waltz the notoriety he has achieved today, effectively explained aspects of the Cold War era but has been increasingly questioned in the post–Cold War era. Ironically, the balance-of-power factor that is so important to the neorealist paradigm can only be explained now if the power variable is changed from military power to economic power. If economics is not considered as the primary power variable, then the United States stands alone as the world's military hegemon, another scenario that should not occur under a neorealist balance-of-power theory.

The institutional theory accepts the neorealist notion of an anarchic system and that at least "bounded rationality" exists among nation-states. The idea that is intriguing and so important to this study is the notion that institutions, whether domestic or international, can constrain the policymaking and agenda-setting efforts of nation-states. This is an idea which is considered absurd in pure neorealist and realist circles.

Whether institutions like the Federal Reserve System constrain policies of nation-states, like the United States, is the question that underlies the examination in Chapters 3, 4, and 5 of the banking practices of the United States and how such practices affect the trade of the United States. The hypothesis—that neorealism fails to adequately explain all aspects of the balance of power of the international system in the post–Cold War era—makes it necessary to demonstrate how the Federal Reserve System, as an institution, has constrained policy in the United States. This hypothesis would give credence to the claim that institutions not only matter in the international system, but that these institutions can constrain and set the policy agenda according to the needs of the institution and the players that the institution benefits.

IMPERIALISM, FREE TRADE, AND THE ROAD TO POWER

In the last several decades, the world's largest economies have increasingly promoted free trade among nations and have pressured more closed economies, such as China and Japan, to liberalize their trade policies to benefit the entire global economy. However, it is interesting how countries that have already achieved economic success, such as Germany, Great Britain, and the United States, have used protectionist policies to fuel their economies when these countries were attempting to build up their own empires.

Imperialism was not, and is not, based on free trade. Even Adam Smith, who is quoted liberally and often used to promote free trade policies, argued that national defense should take priority over economic opulence, giving fodder to those who wished to fuel protectionist policies as well. Smith did argue that Great Britain should engage in free trade in the eighteenth century but that England should protect its shipping industry for the sake of national interest. It is no coincidence that Great Britain's shipping industry was its largest industry at the time (Smith, 1976:484–485).

The United States did not take over as the world's creditor and economic superpower until after World War I when Great Britain lost the ability to continue in that role. Most of the world's gold supply shifted to the United States, and the dollar became the standard of exchange, becoming institutionalized in that function following World War II with the Bretton Woods Agreement. While the gold standard has been abandoned in favor of freely floating exchange rates, the dollar continues to be the currency most often used in worldwide transactions. The foreign exchange market is the largest market in the world, and this will help explain in the next chapter why the Federal Reserve has abandoned the idea of trade balances as essential to national security.

It is interesting to witness how free trade and imperialistic tendencies seem to come in waves, depending on the wealth and power of the countries at the specific time. Great Britain, calling on the world to open up markets to its merchants when it was at the zenith of its wealth and power in the nineteenth and early twentieth centuries, was the European Union's holdout on the question of liberalizing trade and monetary agreements in the late twentieth century.

J. A. Hobson's book *Imperialism* is a scathing critique of the imperialistic policies of Great Britain[5] during the latter part of the nineteenth and early years of the twentieth centuries. Hobson argues that while politicians garnered public support for imperialism under the guise of national interest,[6] the policy actually was detrimental to Great Britain as a whole. The actual beneficiaries were a handful of financial investors and certain manufacturing sectors which benefitted from the expansionist policies, particularly those sectors involved in the war-making process.

Hobson's book, which has something for everyone, is an intellectually stimulating and richly sophisticated work covering topics from international finance to sociology and moral philosophy. While Part 2 of the book is a fascinating account of how imperialism has affected those areas of the world that came under the governance of the British flag, and tests the moral and ethical motives at the very root of those policies, it is Part 1 that I wish to discuss in this section.

Part 1 lays out the economic framework, from Hobson's point of view, for imperialism and also presents the author's economic theory on why imperialism is, in fact, unnecessary, even detrimental to Great Britain's well-being as a nation.

Hobson was a true "redistributive liberalist" in the sense that he believed the oversupply problem associated with imperialism, and capitalism more generally, could be handled by a redistribution of the surplus wealth, thus increasing the domestic consuming power that, in turn, would render unnecessary the forceful takeover policies to create new markets for British goods.

The assumption, sometimes made, that home demand is a fixed amount, and that any commodities made in excess of this amount must find a foreign market, or remain unsold, is quite unwarranted. There is no necessary limit to the quantity of capital and labour that can be employed in supplying the home markets, provided the effective demand for the goods that are produced is so distributed that every increase of production stimulates a corresponding increase of consumption.

Under such conditions a gradual loss of foreign markets could drive more capital and labour into industries supplying home markets; the goods this capital and labour produced would be sold and consumed at home. (Hobson, 1965:29)

Hobson does not argue that Great Britain should become isolationist or that it should halt its external trade,[7] but rather that trade should be in those items which could not be manufactured domestically, or at least manufactured cheaper domestically. Then trade relations should be concentrated on other industrialized countries, where the largest percentage of real trade existed anyway. He claims that this type of trade policy would be much more fruitful than spending vast amounts of money on an expansionist campaign which resulted in a costly venture that did not produce a viable income.[8]

Imperialism seems to be an unprofitable and unwise venture then from both the manufacturers' and the traders' standpoints, but Hobson claims that the investors were making fortunes from foreign investments and were therefore the true forces driving imperialism. These investors made large investments in somewhat risky ventures in the tropical regions and used their influence to persuade the government of Great Britain to guarantee the investments by threat or forcible takeover. The military campaigns that were required to complete these missions forced the government to run a deficit, which the investors gladly funded. The buying up of government debt not only opened up another avenue for investment, but more importantly, it gave these financiers the ability to wield coercive power and manipulate policy.

The book is filled with rich insight on many different levels, but the most important idea to take away from Hobson's work can be found in the chapter entitled "The Economic Taproot of Imperialism." In this chapter, Hobson undermines the logic of imperialism while offering a possible solution to the social ills of society by proposing a way of raising the domestic standard-of-living level through a redistribution of the surplus savings of the rich. He argues:

If, by some economic readjustment, the products which flow from the surplus saving of the rich to swell the overflow streams could be diverted so as to raise the incomes and the standard of consumption of this inefficient fourth,[9] there would be no need for pushful Imperialism, and the cause of social reform would have won its greatest victory. (Hobson, 1965:86)

He argues further that if the standard-of-living level could be brought up to a point where domestic consumption was equal to supply, then the money that was being lost in imperial maintenance and military expenditures could be used to further the productivity power of the nation and support ingenuity and inventiveness within society.

The theory, then, is a theory of domestic underconsumption. If the surplus of the rich could be more equitably distributed, the nation's standard-of-living level, as a whole, would rise. As the consumption power of the poorer sectors of society increased, their propensity to consume would naturally increase. This additional consumption would eat up the excess surplus, giving industry the incentive to produce more while giving the financiers the additional incentive to invest more. As more wealth is produced, more would be distributed and more would be consumed. Hobson argues that the cycle need not have any natural limits and that the wealth created would free humankind to search out the more sophisticated and artistic joys of life.

Hobson predicted that Great Britain's policies would eventually cause the collapse of the great empire's hegemonic dominance, not unlike many of the great empires before her. The United States, the country that would soon replace Great Britain as the economic hegemon and world creditor, also made its fortune through policies opposed to free trade. The United States, like Great Britain and the other great empires before, has called upon the rest of the countries of the world to open up their ports and their markets to U.S. merchants as multinational corporations seek out cheaper labor overseas, a scenario not unlike Hobson's account of British imperialism.

A quick glance at the history of banking and the creation of a central bank in the United States will tell the story of how the country became the financial powerhouse it is today. The story of how the colony under the control of the British Empire in the seventeenth and eighteenth centuries emerged as the world's most powerful empire by the twentieth century is a tale of merchants needing liquidity to trade internationally and calling on the banking industry to provide it. It is also the story of the government using protectionist methods such as tariffs to back up the banking assets so as to give the banking industry the credibility it needed to drive investment.

Bray Hammond's *Banks and Politics in America: From the Revolution to the Civil War* (1985) is a detailed study of the banking history of the United States, with fastidious attention given to the political and cultural forces that led to the tumultuous relationships between the private and public banking sectors with the states and federal government.

Hammond's analysis largely recounts the changing tide of public opinion over whether the establishment of a public bank—a bank which performed many essential functions of modern central banks, particularly control over the monetary supply—was, in fact, constitutional. Hammond correctly acknowledges that raising the constitutionality argument, however valid, was pure rhetoric intended to garner public support for abolishing the federal bank, which placed restrictions on business speculators and competed with state and private banks. The call for laissez-faire in nearly all aspects of society was used as the sounding call for all those who opposed a national bank.[10] The pendulum shifted back and forth numerous times throughout the 170-year period that Hammond describes,[11] and throughout that time two national banks were constructed and dismantled, while only the Civil War could cause a third system of national banks to be reestablished.

The story of a handful of enterprising men getting rich from financial schemes that undermined the nation is nothing out of the ordinary, especially during the period of industrialization. What is unique in Hammond's work, particularly to scholars of American banking history, is his bold argument that the historically accepted notion that banking in the United States evolved from agrarian interests is completely false. The agrarians actually abhorred banking and concluded that it was a dishonest practice. Thomas Jefferson, and later Andrew Jackson, both dismantled the public banks in the United States largely due to these beliefs. These agrarians argued that the only honest living came from the ground. A prevailing view at the time was the following:

The source of wealth was the earth, and the producers thereof were those who tilled it and mined it and fished in its waters. The wealth possessed by bankers and stock-jobbers must have been taken somehow from these toilers. Whence otherwise could it come? (Hammond, 1985:38–39)[12]

The true interests behind the rise of the banking industry in the United States stemmed from the business class, which was desperately in need of a monetary means to engage in international trade, along with badly needed credit from the government to finance wars. Each of the two national banks and the third banking system arose to finance wars, namely the Revolutionary War, the War of 1812, and the Civil War, respectively.

Since it is the function of banks to create money, and since it is characteristic of wars to cost money, the evolution of banking in the United States has received from wars some of its most powerful impulses. (Hammond, 1985:39)

Hammond is insistent that the regulating function of the money supply is the most crucial banking function, but the proponents of the time only considered this function secondary. Even in the end, in an attempt to finance the Civil War, the government was mainly trying to get hold of the monetary supply under a uniform currency.[13] They did not understand fully the importance of its regulatory function, or the main issue that has remained important in today's Federal Reserve system.

Hammond undertakes the awesome task of recounting a volatile time period in American history. He turns on its head the generally accepted notion that the genesis of American banking was debt-ridden agrarian interests and instead brilliantly demonstrates how businessmen and corporations wielded the influence that started the flow of money. "The debtors who owed the most and whose influence was greatest were businessmen; and their complaints were not that their debts were too heavy but that borrowing was not easy enough" (Hammond, 1985:ix). He concludes with the argument that though laissez-faire has continued to dominate our economic and political culture, a government should never relinquish control over the monetary supply. He deems this control an all-important necessity to a country's national interest. "Sovereign and unified control of the monetary system is needed in any economy, whatever freedoms may be proper otherwise" (Hammond, 1985:726).

Hammond's study leaves off at the end of the Civil War with the issue of a central bank in the United States still in question. James Livingston studied the creation of the central banking apparatus we know today as the Federal Reserve System and indicates how the institution is a tool of the wealthy investors it serves.

James Livingston's book (1986) *Origins of the Federal Reserve System: Money, Class, and Corporate Capitalism, 1890–1913* is a detailed analysis of the origins of the U.S. Federal Reserve System. He argues that the banking reforms that resulted in the modern system coincided with the emergence of a new ruling class in America, reflecting the social values and norms of a class-conscious elite that wanted to transform its economic authority into cultural and political authority. This class of business elites was not made up of small entrepreneurs who exhibited the republican ideals so commonly espoused in nineteenth century America. This ruling class was composed of the wealthy capitalists who had emerged from the early stages of the corporate consolidation process.

The populist movement of the late nineteenth century proposed the coinage of free silver and self-regulation of the banking industry, both of which were perceived as threats by the business leaders to industrial productivity and the stability of financial markets. The Federal Reserve System was the ultimate answer to the populist movement; the corporate elites united to uphold their way of life by controlling the savings of the middle class and changing the forum in which issues are debated in the United States today.

Livingston outlines the sequence of events that led to the emergence of the new ruling class. There was a general fall in prices in the late nineteenth century without a comparable fall in labor wages, which resulted in a transfer of income from capital to labor. Meanwhile, the machinery that was being invented was more technologically advanced, allowing for more production, so the factory owners were falling into an overproduction problem. This over-production problem resulted in a lowering of prices and a subsequent decrease in profits.

Capitalists pooled their resources to centralize their power, take away the ability of labor unions to strike, and become more efficient in the only legal forum left available,[14] the corporation. The centralization of industry was intended to limit overproduction, thus stabilizing prices while transferring back to capital the income that labor had been previously "expropriating." Corporate consolidation was viewed as furthering the public interest through a long-term stabilizing and investment effect. In the words of a noted capitalist of the era, Charles R. Flint, "business enterprises are no longer subject to all sorts of unforeseen contingencies. The danger from strikes, lockouts, over-production and ruinous competition is largely eliminated" (Livingston, 1986:61).

The perceived success of the corporate consolidation of America led the capitalists to believe that they could be successful in centralizing the monetary system. It was the idea of consolidating the wealth of the country and controlling it that led the business elite to oppose the free silver argument, thinking that having a currency that more people could afford would increase the money supply and destabilize prices.

Business leaders' defense of the gold standard was, in this sense, a defense of what they conceived to be the natural and necessary alternative to the competitive-entrepreneurial regime, that is, a more concentrated distribution of assets and income that would confer on large firms the power and the duty to manage the price system and the labor process in accordance with a "fair return on capital." (Livingston, 1986:66)

When the crisis of 1907 panicked the nation, the corporate capitalists used the incident to begin pushing for a central bank. They concluded that such a major event could be used to get their ideas on the policy agenda. The competitive banking system, which was supposed to be self-regulating, was viewed as the main culprit of the crisis. The massive and rapid inflation that occurred resulted in a suspension of cash payments by many of the nation's largest banks.

Without centralized control over banking reserves, each bank was forced to compete with all others to protect itself once the crisis had developed;

"competitive hoarding of currency" was the result . . . and it could not be offset by issuing an emergency currency. (Livingston, 1986:173)

Using this scenario, the business leaders wanted to now control policy in what they deemed the national interest.[15]

The Owen-Glass Bill, which culminated in the Federal Reserve Act in 1913, established the new system that the business leaders had been striving for. Livingston argues that these business leaders had a goal of becoming a ruling class and envisioned a long-term plan by which they would achieve it. They defined the cultural, societal, and humanistic needs of an entire country and then educated the populace along those lines to accept that ideology as a technical reality.

Banking reform was the last act in transforming capitalism from a republican, entrepreneurial-competitive system to a centralized trusteeship in which the business elites now controlled the surplus savings of the nation. They institutionalized their ideas and values into the social and political framework of the United States. "These men were . . . committed to remaking capitalism in the United States. The central banking apparatus we know as the Federal Reserve System is a monument to their commitment" (Livingston, 1986:228).

It is interesting to note that this historical account of banking in the United States, particularly the creation of a central bank, demonstrates that while merchants needed more liquidity in the early stages of American history, they needed a banking sector to finance it. When the United States went to war, it needed to issue bonds to finance it, requiring a banking industry in which investors had confidence. And lastly, once trade was deemed as important for the international reputation of the United States, the military was used to open up markets, thus fighting battles for the sake of economic power, not for the sake of military power alone. This instance demonstrates a scenario where the interests of one group, the merchants, induced a nation to call up its war-making machine for the sake of economic gain.

In many instances the corporate capitalists of the nineteenth and twentieth centuries argued that they were working for the national interest, as in the case of centralizing of the nation's reserves so as to smooth out seasonal ebbs and flows in bank reserves which caused instability in the stock market. Whether or not one agrees that actions and policies promoted by corporate elites were in the national interest, one fact remains certain: they created an institution that then changed the way the whole world eventually did business—a situation that clearly indicates that institutions do matter, and can constrain policy, both domestically and internationally.

THE SHAPING OF THE REPUBLIC: A PARALLEL OF CENTRALIZED POWER

In the United States, the notion of popular sovereignty has at its foundation a deep-rooted philosophical concern for the issue of accountability. The debate over accountability stems from the question of who holds power, and from where those who hold power derive the authority to wield it. There are certainly legal and cultural factors involved that lead back to the founding of the country; however, the issues may have been best brought to light by the debate between the Federalists and the Anti-federalists which preceded the ratification of the Constitution. Professors Bruce Miroff and Todd Swanstrom at the University at Albany, State University of New York, and Raymond Seidelman at Sarah Lawrence College (1995) have written a unique text entitled *The Democratic Debate* for their introductory course in American politics. The text is unique because it addresses the debate between the Federalists and Anti-Federalists and rekindles an important part of U.S. history that has either long since been forgotten or has escaped the history books altogether. The main issues that this debate raised were differences in how the Federalists and Anti-federalists viewed representation and human nature and what effects adoption of the Constitution, and hence the establishment of a republic, would have on the future of the United States.

This issue is applicable here for numerous reasons, but most importantly because the debates between centralized and decentralized banking parallel closely both the reasoning and time lines involved here, and because accountability is a major factor when dealing with a bureaucracy such as the Fed. The Federalists did not think that the people would best be served by a true representative-style democracy; such a system would prove to be unwieldy an inefficient. The Federalists thought that a trustee style government should be implemented so that a smaller, more qualified group could run the government and serve on behalf of the rest of the citizens. The corporate capitalists made a similar argument when calling for the end of the self-regulating banking system in favor of a centralized system.

The Federalists, often characterized under the beliefs and writings of James Madison, viewed people with a sense of distrust, fearing that the selfish and contentious ways of human nature would lead to rebellious factions and the abuse of minority viewpoints. A large republic, represented by educated and well-trained officials, was believed to be the answer to revolting factions. The public officials would serve in a trustee capacity, where the knowledge and expertise of each representative would be relied upon to make decisions that were in the best interest of the nation and its citizens. In *Federalist No. 10*, James Madison explained that this process of representation would

refine and enlarge the public views by passing them through the medium of a chosen body of citizens, whose wisdom may best discern the true interest of their country and whose patriotism and love of justice will be least likely to sacrifice it to temporary or partial consideration. (Rossiter, 1961:82)

Again, Madison's rationale is similar to the views espoused by the corporate capitalists on centralizing the nation's savings because they knew how to deal with the surplus in a way that would foster investment and growth.

The separation of powers that was built into the Constitution was put in place to prohibit any branch of government or particular individual from engaging in tyrannical behavior. These separations would most likely not have been implemented if there had not been such fierce debate waged by their proponents. In this respect, which will be discussed in more detail in the next chapter, the Fed did not have checks and balances to the same degree as those built into the structure of government by the Constitution, and this is largely because the corporate capitalists created such a strong constituency of the most wealthy and powerful people of the era that most of the opposition's viewpoints were kept off the agenda.

The Anti-federalists' viewpoints, often characterized by the writings of Brutus, a penname for a gentleman who was believed to be a judge from upstate New York, favored smaller republics with representatives serving in a delegate role, where the representative would be a voice of the people, voting in accordance with, and as a mirror of, the will of the constituent majority. The Anti-federalists believed that there needed to be more representatives, who would be limited to shorter terms of office than outlined by the Federalists and that there would be limits to the number of terms a representative could serve. They wanted more participation by ordinary Americans rather than just elites, feeling that the people could govern themselves in a just manner if given the opportunity, allowing the majorities to arrive at decisions stemming from similar interests (Miroff, 1995:39).

The Federalists believed that the format outlined in the Constitution would protect minority interests and claimed that a more popular role in participation, which was favored by the Anti-federalists, would lead to contentious factions which would crush minority interests and lead to tyranny (Rossiter, 1961:320–325).

The Anti-federalists countered by arguing that more participation from the public was the only protection the people had from office holders turning into a group of elites who ruled the government in the form of an established aristocracy (Miroff, 1995: 320).

As the debate continued, the Federalists argued that the bicameral Congressional format would serve as a compromising model, where members serving in the Senate could serve in a trustee role while the members of the House, the number based on proportional representation, would allow for a larger voice for the people (Rossiter, 1961: 330–336).

The Anti-federalists argued that the areas of representation were so large that the nature of the political game, and the social and financial resources necessary to campaign for office, required a vast network of high-profile contacts virtually unavailable to the poor and middle classes. The other argument noted that an increasing representation based on the constant growth of the nation, would eventually create an institution with so many members that virtually no public business could be transacted (Miroff, 1995:320). They were right in this regard, as it turns out, since Congress eventually decided that the number of members in the House of Representatives had to be capped.

Brutus' fear that a large republic would alienate the people it governed—and that its representatives would create an aristocracy—ultimately lost out to the Federalists' arguments, although there were many concessions due to compromises in the rich debate.

POWER AND THE POLICYMAKING ARENA

Given the fact that as a society we have accepted the separation of powers doctrine and have given the theory "teeth" by ratification of the Constitution and subsequent legislative enactments and court rulings, we seem to have endorsed the idea that power should be in the hands of the legislative branch (in the sense of decision-making ability or public policy making, which is typically summed up by Nelson Polsby's conceptions of "who participates, who gains and loses, and who prevails in decision-making") (Polsby, 1963: 55). Legislators are directly elected by the people, thus responsible to their constituency for their actions.

The guidelines have already been established on how power is generally measured by the majority of international relations scholars and policy makers, comprising the neorealist school of thought, meaning that the more military might a nation possesses the more powerful it is; but there is a much different set of debates in the current literature on power and participation, theories that are meant to be generalizable to the larger domestic and international policy arenas. The reason that it is important to study the role that power plays in participation is because the institutionalists believe that institutions matter, and institutions embody the interests and ideas of the people they represent and benefit. There are different substantive and methodological positions that explain representation either as it exists in its current form or as the current model may affect political participation (or nonparticipation). I will explain why participation/nonparticipation is power for some while decision making is power for others. Two of the classics in academic literature that seem to represent the two main opposing paradigms these areas are Robert Dahl's *Who Governs?* (1961), and John Gaventa's *Power and Powerlessness* (1982).

Staying with the Federalists/Anti-federalists theme for fluidity, Dahl seems to argue from the Federalists' perspective on the notion of representation because he believes in the centralized institutional framework and maintains that stability is more important than popular participation. He argues that the public should not be overly involved in government except through the electoral process. He, like the Federalists, believes that too much participation by the masses would lead to instability. However, the fact that the people have not used up their potential resources (he uses the term "slack resources"), keeps representatives in check. He argues that the basic tenets and beliefs of Americans in the "creed," or democratic values, forces those in power to abide by certain principles and acts as a governor to self-interested ambitions which could lead to dictatorial or abusive policies toward the populace (Dahl, 1961:95).

Power, for Dahl, is the ability to make policy decisions. He operationalizes this concept in his famous essay. "My intuitive idea of power is something like this: A has power over B to the extent that he can get B to do something that B would not otherwise do" (Dahl, 1969:80). Dahl was trained as a behavioralist, so power is more an action than an invisible structure. He has to be able to see it; it must have some sort of empirical element to it before it exists.

Pluralism to Dahl is basically that there are those that participate and those that do not. Those that do not have the ability to mobilize and make their wishes and concerns known. He concedes that only a handful of political leaders actually forge policy, but he believes that these leaders are held in restraint by the people—or their potential to mobilize—from going too far and obtaining too much power (Dahl, 1961:315–325).

Gaventa argues more from the Anti-federalist point of view in regards to representation and power. Gaventa's research demonstrates how empirical studies can be combined with theory-driven models under a structural research design. The main objective of structuralism is to explain the direct variables rather than the indirect variable, which is the structure of the system. Behavioralism studies the motivation behind behavior, while structuralism makes assumptions about motivation.

Gaventa researches the question of why some people, the powerless, acquiesce rather than rebel under certain conditions. He used a case study of coal miners in the Appalachian Valley as a research model to make his theory generalizable to why powerless groups fail to rebel. The system under which the people in the Appalachian Valley lived, Gaventa argued, caused the inequalities and obstacles to rebellion. Gaventa went to great lengths to provide quantitative as well as qualitative data, ranging from personal interviews to statistical computations, in his attempt to prove that the structure of the system caused the exploitation of the coal miners, whether by the corporate elites or union bosses.

Such a study has a parallel to both the neorealist structural balance-of-power model—in that the system dictates the actions of the unit of analysis—and the institutional model—in that the agenda-setting of policy ideas, actual policymaking, and implementation of policies are all largely constrained by the actions of the group or institution that has the wealth, information, influence, and political resources to mobilize.

Gaventa is a structuralist, more like the Marxists than the functionalists, so for him, power lies in the structure itself. Unlike Dahl, he is not only concerned with measuring the conspicuous, but he also attempts to make the unobservable more observable. Gaventa, like Dahl, agreed that there was stability in the current system, but unlike Dahl, Gaventa asserts that the stability is detrimental. Gaventa argues that the structure of the system caused the exploitation of the people in the Appalachian Valley, leaving them voiceless and powerless (Gaventa, 1982:11).

Another major difference between the two is that Dahl only examines those who actually participate or make decisions. If someone does not participate, then there is nothing for Dahl to analyze, and that person is then excluded from the study. Gaventa argues that by ignoring nondecisions the researcher is missing a great deal (Gaventa, 1982:12).

Gaventa's study clearly reflects the sentiments of the Antifederalists in that the structure has created an elite class that rules. This structure has left the masses voiceless and powerless in a system in which their representatives do not represent their needs, and it has rendered the masses incapable of mobilizing to change the system. Because of their inability to create change, the masses do not participate. Therefore, the structure creates stability through nonparticipation, which stems from a lack of representation (Gaventa, 1982:17–20).

The Federal Reserve, and the interests it represents, may be viewed as the elites who dictate economic policy. The secrecy of the meetings held by the Board of Governors, where monetary policy is created, leaves the general public out of the agenda-setting loop and thus requires the citizenry to sit back and assume that the Fed is working in the nation's best interests. This phenomenon can also explain why foreign policy in the United States is created and implemented largely in realist terms; the public and the policy makers believe that the zero-sum game being played out in the international system leaves nation-states no choice but to pursue military dominance in the name of national interest. The perceived inability to change the way the world works is one reason why members of both major political parties in the United States continue to support the military-industrial complex.

At this point in the chapter, I would like to examine the question of whether power can be wielded without the knowledge or consent of the governed. C. Wright Mills (1956) answered this question outright in *The Sociological Imagination* over four decades ago, stating:

We cannot assume today that men must in the last resort be governed by their own consent. Among the means of power that now prevail is the power to manage and manipulate the consent of men. That we do not know the limits of such power—and that we hope it does have limits— does not remove the fact that much power today is successfully employed without the sanction of the reason or the conscience of the obedient. (Mills, 1956:40–41)

Peter Bachrach and Morton S. Baratz (1962) also argue in their famous work "The Two Faces of Power," that pluralists—remembering here that the pluralists are the neorealists of American public policy—miss important issues by measuring power in Dahl's traditional format of A makes B do something B would not ordinarily do (Dahl, 1969:95). To the extent that B believes in the process, even under Dahl's own hypothesis, it does not seem as though B would understand that he/she is having power wielded over him/her without consent. Bachrach and Baratz state:

Of course power is exercised when A participates in the making of decisions that affect B. But power is also exercised when A devotes his energies to creating or reinforcing social and political values and institutional practices that limit the scope of the political process to public consideration of only those issues which are comparatively innocuous to A. To the extent that A succeeds in doing this, B is prevented, for all practical purposes, from bringing to the fore any issues that might in their resolution be seriously detrimental to A's set of preferences. (Bachrach, 1962:948)

To hammer the point home, E. E. Schattschneider, in his classic treatise *The Semi-Sovereign People*, wrote:

All forms of political organization have a bias in favor of the exploitation of some kinds of conflict and the suppression of others because organization is the mobilization of bias. Some issues are organized into politics while others are organized out. (Schattschneider, 1975:71)

Gaventa lays out the literature for what he deems the three dimensions of power. I have spoken about the first and the third somewhat, and the second is basically Bachrach and Baratz's second face of power, which is primarily the pluralist argument but with the added mobilization of bias. I will now list some of the scholars who have done work in each of these dimensions.

Because the first dimension of power places "its emphasis on observable conflict in decision-making arenas, power may be understood primarily by looking at who prevails in bargaining over the resolution of key issues" (Gaventa, 1982:13–14). As mentioned earlier, Robert Dahl and Nelson Polsby are the two scholars most closely linked with this dimension. The mechanisms of power that are wielded are largely political resources such as "votes, jobs, influence—that can be brought by political actors to the bargaining game" (Gaventa, 1982:14).

The second dimension of power, largely supported by the writings of E. E. Schattschneider, but later formally developed by Bachrach and Baratz, adds mobilization of bias to the list of resources, whereby "power is exercised not just upon participants within the decision-making process but also towards the exclusion of certain participants and issues altogether" (Bachrach and Baratz, 1962:641–651). Michael Parenti found in his study that "one of the most important aspects of power is not to prevail in a struggle, but to predetermine the agenda of struggle—to determine whether certain questions ever reach the competition stage" (Parenti, 1970:501–530). In their respective studies Lester Salamon and Stephen Van Evera (1973) and Eric Wolf (1969) found that fear of sanctions and retaliation of powerful elites kept the powerless in their studies from rebelling. This is where non-decisions enter this dimension of power.

The third dimension of power has been supported by sociologists and communication scholars, among others, but finds supporters in C. Wright Mills (1956), Steven Lukes (1974), Gaventa (1982), and Antonio Gramsci (1957). Gaventa describes this dimension where

their identification . . . involves specifying the means through which power influences, shapes or determines conceptions of the necessities, possibilities, and strategies of challenge in situations of latent conflict. . . . It may involve, in short, locating the power processes behind the social construction of meanings and patterns that serve to get B to act and believe in a manner in which B otherwise might not, to A's benefit and B's detriment. (Gaventa, 1982:15–16)

Pluralists, and rational actor scholars have often argued that political participation is a result of political awareness. Anthony Downs (1957) argues in *An Economic Theory of Democracy* that all participation or nonparticipation can be traced to utility-maximization, or in more recent terminology, "Do the benefits of action outweigh the costs of participation?" If benefits do not outweigh the costs, such as he concludes for "indifferent" citizens, "indifferent citizens [will] always abstain" (Downs, 1957:261).

The third dimension of power approach counters the above-mentioned argument and states instead that "participation itself . . . increases political consciousness" (Gaventa, 1982:17). This argues that as the governed have less opportunity to participate, they may be less and less inclined to do so. This is the dangerous point where the governed have become powerless and where those who govern are no longer accountable to those they govern. Gramsci summed it up many years ago, stating: "It can reach the point where the contradiction of conscience will not permit any decision, any choice, and produce a state of moral and political passivity" (Gramsci, 1957:67). Has this not occurred in modern international politics and economics as well? The person or country that advocates any type of system other than a democratic, free-market economy, despite whether the fit is a good one or not, is often criminalized and ostracized by the international community, leading many transitional and developing countries down dangerous paths.

Now that some of the cultural and legal aspects that explain the issues of power and accountability in a representative democracy have been outlined—as well as the idea that power is not necessarily derived from the people, thus questioning the whole idea of representation and accountability in a federal republic—it is time to understand how bureaucracies such as the Federal Reserve System fit into such a scene.

There are some social scientists and policy scholars, like James Q. Wilson (1975), who do not necessarily believe that bureaucracies are unaccountable or that they really create much policy. He argues in "The Rise of the Bureaucratic State" that while the bureaucratic state has grown into a vast machine, it is still largely under the control of Congress, despite their claims to the opposite. He claims that:

If the Founding Fathers were to return to review their handiwork, they would no doubt be staggered by the size but they would not, I suspect, think that our Constitutional arrangements for managing these enterprises have proved defective or that there had occurred, as a result of the creation of these vast bureaus, an important shift in the locus of political authority. (Wilson, 1975:87)

Wilson further concludes that the bureaucratic state, referring to the United States, did not grow in order for bureaucrats to usurp more power for themselves, as many organizational theorists might argue, or because of the complexity of modern times. He argues:

It did not result simply from increased specialization, the growth of industry, or the imperialistic designs of the bureaus themselves. Before the second decade of this century, there was no federal bureaucracy wielding substantial discretionary powers. That we have one now is the result of political decisions made by elected representatives. . . . The particularistic and localistic nature of American democracy has created a particularistic and client-serving administration. If our bureaucracy often serves special interest and is subject to no central direction, it is because our legislature often serves special interest and is subject to no central leadership. . . . Congress could change what it has devised, but there is little reason to suppose it will. (Wilson, 1975:103)

Wilson is certainly correct in that Congress does have the authority to legislate mandates in how the Federal Reserve makes policy but has used this authority only sparingly since the Fed's creation in 1913. The deep pockets of those in the industry that the Federal Reserve represents and regulates have been successful at keeping policymaking autonomy in the hands of the bankers, and out of the hands of Congress. Certainly two important reasons that Congress leaves most of the policymaking authority in the hands of the Board of Governors are (1) the philosophical issues discussed earlier in this chapter that surrounded the debates over the ratification of the Constitution and (2) the events that led to the creation of the Federal Reserve System. The belief in the "trustee" system, that those who are better informed and know the industry should be making the

Table 4.1
Major Legislative Mandates

Legislative Mandates	Intended Results
Federal Reserve Act of 1913	Provide elastic currency, thereby fulfilling the role of the lender of last resort so as to help avoid financial panics and bank runs.
The Employment Act of 1946	Promote maximum employment opportunities and foster production and purchasing power.
Full Employment and Balanced Growth Act of 1978	Promote maximum employment, stable prices, and moderate long-term interest rates.

Source: Federal Reserve Bank of San Francisco, 1996b.

decisions for and on behalf of the larger general population, is a strong influence in the financial arena in the United States. However, if Congress was truly worried about the trade deficit, it could legislate a mandate that a trade balance is the goal of Federal Reserve monetary policy. Table 4.1 lists some of the major legislative mandates handed down by Congress.

There are other theorists, like Theodore Lowi (1979), who believe that the Supreme Court ought to rule unconstitutional any policy legislation that does not specifically outline the details of implementation, thus taking away discretionary powers from government agencies. This is the same view held by many monetarists, like Milton Friedman, when it comes to the Federal Reserve making monetary policy.

CONCLUSION

The Federal Reserve has gained power over the years and has successfully created an agency where the agenda is set and policies are often created behind closed doors. The general public has very little knowledge of what the Fed actually does, beyond the periodic interest rate shifts, pays almost no attention to its actions outside of interest rate management, and assumes that the Fed is working for and on behalf of the national interest. The banking industry recently won its battle to remove many of the regulatory measures that bankers have long argued made it difficult for them to compete in the new global economy by getting Congress to repeal the Glass-Steagall Act of 1933. The Federal Reserve played a major role in getting the law repealed, once again demonstrating how the banking industry's leading institution is working on its behalf. The Glass-Steagall Act of 1933 was passed in order to mitigate the risk of banking and economic crises. According to a November 5, 1999 article in the *New York Times* by Stephen Labaton, some insiders like the senator from New York, Charles E. Schumer, Democrat, indicated that the move was in the nation's best interests. He stated:

We could find London or Frankfurt or years down the road Shanghai becoming the financial capital of the world. . . . There are many reasons for this bill, but first and foremost is to ensure that U.S. financial firms remain competitive.

It is interesting that the law was first enacted to ensure the long-term health of the economy, and that it has been repealed for the same reason.

Will the deregulation, which allows banks to merge with other financial industries, actually benefit the citizens of the United States as a whole—as the lower costs of doing business lead to lower interest rates and insurance premiums, for example—or will the eventual lack of competition as fewer companies are left to compete for a larger share of the market cause rates to increase? There is certainly no doubt that the financial sector will cash in on the deal, but only time will tell whether or not the consumer will be as fortunate over the long run. The move carries some risks of repeating the mistakes of the past, risks that proponents indicate no longer exist due to tighter transparency rules and a Federal Reserve that is determined to stave off economic crisis.

The fact is that the financial sector was not making as much money as it could have. Greater risk means greater chance of earning higher returns, but as we learned from the savings and loan debacle, it can also be a recipe for disaster.

This chapter has demonstrated how one industry institutionalized its interests into an organization that now serves as its political arm in the policymaking arena. This group of savvy businessmen and women have made real changes in the way the United States and the rest of the world works. Cold War era balance-of-power systems theorists will struggle to explain this post–Cold War phenomenon.

First and foremost, the most important actors in the new struggle for power are not necessarily nation-states, and therefore the type of power they strive for has changed as well.

Secondly, this chapter has demonstrated that institutions do matter, and that they can and do constrain nation-state policy, demonstrating that power can be wielded, and policy promulgated, by small groups of participants that are largely unaccountable by democratic means.

Chapter 5

Monetary Policy,
Foreign Exchange, and Trade

INTRODUCTION

The economies of the world's nation-states are growing increasingly more interdependent as the marketplace for trade has expanded in a global fashion. While trade seems to be one of the buzzwords of policy makers, politicians, the media, corporations, and labor unions, this chapter will question the role of a seemingly nonactive trade policy from the standpoint of the U.S. Federal Reserve System. A comparative approach will be employed to identify certain characteristics that have been successful for one of the world's most effective banking institutions in recent decades and to examine how the U.S. Federal Reserve should implement these objectives into its mission statement so that the United States can continue to thrive in the global economy of the twenty-first century.

The country, or rather the banking system, that will serve as the comparison model is the German Bundesbank. Germany and the United States, while differing in size, have quite similar standard-of-living levels when measured by GDP per capita, private and public consumption, and GDP growth.

The central bank of Germany—prior to its somewhat diminished role under the European Monetary Union, which went into effect on January 1, 1999—was committed in its support for international trade, particulary domestic exportation, without the obstacles of political restraint and regulation to hinder its policy objectives. The reader will discover why the role of the Bundesbank is so important in this regard, independent of other issues where the two political and economic systems may differ.

The U.S. Federal Reserve is largely independent and has the power to formulate monetary policy, which in theory could empower it to formulate trade policy in a manner which promotes a balance of trade.

Some economists and policy makers have argued that a congressional mandate should be issued to force the Fed to make trade balances a priority. Such a mandate could provide a shelter from political pressure when the Fed needs to make unpopular decisions for the long-term benefit of the country. Others argue for more independence and less government oversight and regulation in the banking sector. This type of autonomy would allow the Fed to actively create trade policy and engage in foreign exchange rate management practices that are often created in conjunction with the U.S. Treasury now.

However, the Fed is supposed to be an organization that acts in the national interest, looking through the rational actor lense; does the United States really want to give more autonomy to an institution that already seems to be acting in some ways contrary to those interests? The last chapter outlined reasons against such autonomy; and as the Fed's role as a domestic institution is analyzed further in this chapter, the evidence will show that less autonomy and more accountability should be instigated.

An example of a policy that has been promoted by many economists, and that will be developed later in this chapter, is the policy of inflating the dollar. This policy has been theorized as one possible solution to balancing the U.S. trade deficit and is a policy that many central banks around the world use when necessary, including the German Bundesbank.

The role of central banks should not be to support a specific industry or even to shore up the international economy, and "is not to earn a profit as such, but rather to influence the foreign exchange value of their currency in a manner that will be beneficial to the interests of their citizens" (Eiteman, 1995:85).

A strong central bank with a mandate to create trade policy consistent with a balance of trade could devalue the dollar in an attempt to promote a healthy, long-term economic outlook while being able to withstand political pressures from congressional constituencies who feel the short-term pains of the devalued dollar. This is the type of policymaking shelter that the German central bank encompasses, and it has led to Germany's longstanding financial stability. It was an absolute must for a country that saw the largest inflationary explosion in the history of the world during the Weimar Republic. Why has the same scenario not been played out in the United States?

It is quite possible that the scenarios are different because the Federal Reserve is not acting as a tool of the nation-state, but rather it is acting on behalf of the industry it regulates and serves, the banking industry. Changes in the global economy have created the need for a strong dollar so as to create cheap imports and keep labor prices down overseas. Another key element is that the foreign exchange market continues to be the largest market in the world, and a strong dollar means a huge windfall for the financial sector. As Robert Keohane and Helen Milner note in *Internationalization and Domestic Politics*, "institutions reflect the preferences of powerful actors: when actors' preferences change and new policies are pursued, institutional change is likely to follow" (Keohane and Milner, 1996:244).

THE PROBLEM

When Bill Clinton was elected president, he announced at the outset of his first term that the U.S. economy should be ranked in importance alongside national security and appointed an economic council to help accomplish this objective. He also emphasized the importance of trade, yet the trade deficit increased nearly every year he was in office.

Samuel Huntington emphasized the importance of economic policy in regards to the changing post Cold War world. In this new environment . . . military capabilities are likely to be less important than they have been in the past. Economic measures will be central . . . ; diplomacy and economics will be crucial. . . . the promotion of U.S. strategic interests will involve not only foreign and defense policy but also domestic policy on the budget, taxes, subsidies, industrial policy, science and technology, child care, education, and other topics. (Wolf, 1995:16)

The U.S. trade deficit, which continues to reach record levels nearly every year, is largely the main driver of the current account deficit. These annual deficits are rendering the American standard-of-living level increasingly dependent on the investments of foreign nation-states.

The alarming rate at which the trade deficits increased throughout the decade of the 1990s and into the 2000s is cause for concern. In order to finance the debt that the United States owes to other countries, it is forced to either borrow or allow these countries to invest further. Where as U.S. military prowess has always allowed it to wield influence in international matters, many security specialists such as Donald Snow (1995) in his book *National Security: Defense Policy for a New International Order* argue that due to global economic interdependence among nation-states, war is less likely to erupt over economic issues. However, whether or not interdependency keeps trading nations from going to war, the psychological realm of security is being threatened in America, which still often employs a protectionist attitude toward trade policy, even if its policy makers are slow to admit it.

When we buy more goods and services from foreigners than we sell to them, we must give the foreigners something else to cover the difference. What we give them is assets. The U.S. trade deficit . . . [is] financed by a steady sale of American assets—stocks, bonds, real estate, and, increasingly, whole corporations to foreigners. (Krugman, 1995:48)

As the American market pleads for foreign succor to finance its standard of living, there is a growing concern among Americans in regard to the decreasing superpower role that the United States plays in the international market and an uneasiness that the United States is actually dependent on foreign markets to keep financially afloat.

The question then arises as to how the trade deficit should be controlled in the United States and in the other industrialized countries of the world, all of which now play very significant roles in the new globally interdependent economy. This chapter will address that question by advancing the theme that the central banks of nation-states should be the institutions actively involved in controlling monetary policy in a mode which facilitates a balance of trade.

A comparative approach will be used to examine and conceptualize the possible trade policy roles of central banking institutions. The countries that will be specifically examined are the United States and Germany. The European Union will also be discussed as it prepared to meet the Maastricht Treaty requirements which were necessary for economic integration on January 1, 1999. We will also examine why Germany proposed that the new system of central banks should resemble a model formulated after the German Bundesbank.

Germany and the United States have strong similarities that make them attractive choices for this analysis. Both nations are major players in the economic and international trade arenas, both of these countries' central banks actively engage in monetary policy strategies that are concentrated on inflation-fighting measures, and the currencies of both countries are two of the three strongest and most heavily traded currencies in the world (prior to the establishment of the euro).

The area where Germany and the United States differ dramatically is on the weight placed on trade balances. The promotion of a strong U.S. dollar, and an inflation-fighting policy by the Federal Reserve that aims mostly at consumer prices, almost ensures a trade deficit under freer trade agreements that are being adopted worldwide.

One other major difference between the two countries is that while both countries have as a matter of historical fact consistently run annual budget deficits (though the United States turned this around in the late 1990s), Germany rarely experienced trade deficits during the years that led up to European integration.

Trade is becoming increasingly more important for the economies of the world's nation-states. The central banks of these nations, therefore, must actively engage in monetary policies that facilitate a balance of trade, not only for the good of that particular country, but also for a healthy balance in the world's economy. The U.S. Federal Reserve should learn from Germany's success, and implement trade policies into its list of objectives. Germany, on the other hand, should be careful not to compromise its successful central banking policies as it moves toward complete economic integration with the European Union. When Helmut Kohl was defeated in 1998, the electorate was stating that Germany, as the economic foundation of the EU, still has a responsibility to its own citizens, an issue which future leaders may have to deal with if the EMU does not benefit Germany more positively than Germany could have on its own.

BRIEF HISTORY AND CURRENT POLICIES

From the end of World War II through August 1971, the world's exchange rates were regulated and promoted through the International Monetary Fund (IMF) and the World Bank. Forty-four of the world's largest industrial nations signed an agreement in Bretton Woods, New Hampshire, known as the Bretton Woods Agreement, which tied the U.S. dollar to its gold reserves, since it held the largest reserves, and all the other nations' currencies were regulated according to the fluctuation of the dollar in the international marketplace. Nations were not allowed to alter their own exchange rates by more than plus or minus one percent of the normal going rate.

As the other nations of the world, such as Japan and Germany, gained on the U.S. economy, they wanted more independence in regard to their exchange rates, or else wanted their own currencies to set the norm due to the continued weakening value of the dollar, at least in international perception. With large foreign aid projects such as the Marshall Plan and aid to third world countries, the U.S. economy was softening while countries like Japan and Germany were benefitting from the foreign aid programs and their productivity levels were growing at impressive rates. On August 15, 1971, President Nixon abolished the Bretton Woods plan and called for a freely floating market. With that, each nation-state was free to dictate its own exchange rates.

The U.S. Federal Reserve system is comprised of seven governors, a twelve-member Advisory Council and a twelve-member Open Market Committee. Each governor is nominated by the president and confirmed by the U.S. Senate, serving one term which consists of fourteen years. The president appoints the chair and vice chair; each serves four-year terms that are open for reappointment. The Federal Reserve outlines its own objectives and purpose in the following format. It

- manages money and operates at the center of the nation's financial system,
- keeps the wheels of business rolling with coin, currency, and payment services, such as electronic funds transfer and check clearing,
- supervises and regulates a large share of the nation's banking and financial system,
- administers banking and finance-related consumer protection laws. (Federal Reserve Bank of San Franciso, 1996c)

The main objective of the Federal Reserve is to manage the nation's money supply. The Federal Reserve, or any other official central banking institution, did not exist in the United States until 1913. However, there were national banks that performed similar functions, and some local banking institutions did attempt to perform some rudimentary central banking activities early on in the nation's history, but this decentralized approach tended to create sporadic and uneven growth patterns in regional economies. The dysfunctional banking system stimulated public apprehension, providing the catalyst which finally resulted in the great panic of 1907.

"In 1913, after considerable debate, Congress passed the Federal Reserve Act" (Federal Reserve Bank of San Francisco, 1996c), which created the first official central banking institution in the United States. The Federal Reserve has become the supreme management and regulatory institution of the U.S. money supply ever since its enactment. The Fed maintains that

money and credit are the very lifeblood of the economy, and the Fed's job is to keep the nation's economic blood pressure under control. Too much money drives consumer prices up and causes inflation. Too little money idles workers and equipment and causes recession. (Federal Reserve Bank of San Francisco, 1996c)

The Federal Reserve has an erratic history: initially it created monetary policy, then became an organization that merely carried out prescribed technical functions, and currently creates monetary policy again.

Milton Friedman (1962) was an active supporter of the Fed merely carrying out technical functions in order to achieve a steady growth of the money supply, and he also argued in his book *Capitalism and Freedom* that floating exchange rates would cure the balance of payment problems associated with trade. In the early 1980s under Paul Volcker (and a floating international exchange rate regime), the Fed changed its priorities to merely achieving monetary targets, thus seeming to give Friedman's supporters their victory. However, many economists look back at this period and believe that the Fed was purposely hiding behind this policy so it could strangle the excessive inflation. This gave the country the painful medicine it needed while allowing the Fed to escape the blame since it was now merely a bureaucratic machine that was supposed to hit monetary aggregates. The Fed subsequently shed the role of its technical duties for a more active monetary policy role again immediately upon the successful turnaround of the U.S. economy (Krugman, 1995:66).

The management of the money supply is known as monetary policy. The importance of monetary policy has lifted the Federal Reserve to the stature of arguably the most powerful institution in the world. In theory, while slow to take effect in and of itself, experts estimate that monetary policy can require anywhere from six months to two years to have an effect. However, monetary policy normally has a quicker response time than fiscal policy, which refers to Congressional legislation enacted for the purpose of either slowing or stimulating economic activity. The responsiveness of monetary policy is one of the factors supporting the argument that the Federal Reserve, and other central banking institutions abroad, should actively engage in creating trade policy through interest rate management rather than leaving trade policy strictly in the hands of the executive and legislative branches of government.

Critics of fiscal policy argue that it often aggravates problems in the economy rather than solves them, not that many critics of monetary policy would argue that it is any different, since monetary policy is merely gambling on the fact that interest rates will induce borrowing or saving. However, fiscal policy does have to clear many time-consuming obstacles because getting legislation through legislative bodies, such as the U.S. Congress, is never an easy task no matter what the circumstances. In the example of a recession, by the time legislation is created and enacted, the recession may have already corrected itself. The "Economic Stimulus Package" passed by Congress in the spring of 2002 is a perfect example. Most economists agree that the national recession ended in the late fall or early winter of 2001, long before the legislation was ever signed into law. Any antirecession legislation could cause the economy to overheat, thus resulting in inflation.

The Federal Reserve wields three basic tools in its struggle to manage the economy: its ability to influence "the availability of money and credit reserve requirements, the discount rate, and open market operations" (Federal Reserve Bank of San Francisco, 1996a).

The reserve requirements deal with the percentage of any given bank's deposits that it is required by law to keep in reserve, thus changing the amount of money that a bank can make available for lending purposes. This reserve requirement is called the reserve requirement ratio. Increasing the reserve requirement ratio tightens the amount of money that can be borrowed, thus decreasing the flow of currency into the economy. Lowering the reserve requirement ratio accordingly allows a larger portion of a bank's reserves to be borrowed, thus increasing the flow of money into the economy (Federal Reserve Bank of San Francisco, 1996a).

The reserve requirement is one of the most powerful yet understudied mechanisms of central banking. It ensures that banks have enough money on hand or, in the case of the United States, on reserve in an account with the Federal Reserve, to handle daily transactions that are expected. This system of reserve requirements also breeds another market of its own called the federal funds market, consisting mostly of commercial banking institutions, though some government security traders enter this market as well. When one bank is low on reserves and another bank has excess reserves the bank with the excess can loan money to the bank that is in need of funds to meet the reserve requirement. The rate that these institutions charge to borrow from one another is called the federal funds rate. Usually the discount rate serves as the ceiling for this rate since banks can also borrow from the Fed (Board of Governors of the Federal Reserve System, 1963:49).

When the Federal Reserve System raises the reserve requirement, it can expand or contract the money supply. A 5 percent increase or decrease in the reserve requirement can increase or decrease the money supply in the whole system by as much as a third (Board of Governors of the Federal Reserve System, 1963:52). This is a complicated process because banks tend to loan out all available funds beyond the reserve requirement, and what is known as the multiplying effect of bank reserves actually allows banks to "make" money. This effect occurs when one person invests money in a bank, making funds available for the bank to loan back out, minus the reserve requirement. That loan will very likely be taken and put into a bank account somewhere else, where that bank can turn around and loan the money out, minus the reserve requirement. This concept can be explained in a scenario described in *The Federal Reserve System: Purposes and Functions*, where $100 is deposited into a checking account where there is a 20 percent reserve requirement (see Exhibit 1 in Appendix A).

The member bank at which $100 is deposited needs to hold $20 in required reserves . . . and it may lend or invest the remaining $80.

Suppose that all the money is lent. The amount lent is first credited to the borrower's deposit account. This money is then paid out at once by the borrower to someone who deposits it at another bank. The cash holdings and newly created deposits of the first bank are thus drawn down and transferred to a second bank.

The second bank receives $80 in cash reserves and in new deposits; it holds $16 as required reserve against the deposit received and can lend the remaining $64. Similarly, the borrower here may draw down the additional newly created deposit at once, but the funds will merely be shifted to a third bank, which in turn can lend 80 percent of $64, thereby adding a further $51.20 to deposits.

This sequence can be traced through many banks until $500 of demand deposits have grown out of the original $100 deposit. On the asset side of their books, the banks hold $100 in reserves (20 percent of $500) and $400 in loan or investment paper.

Thus, an individual bank does not lend more than it receives, but the banking system as a whole expands by a multiple of the new reserve funds made available to it. The fact that individual member banks are required to hold only a fraction of their deposits as reserves and the fact that payments made with the proceeds of bank loans are eventually redeposited with banks make it possible for additional reserve funds, as they are deposited and invested through the banking system as a whole, to generate deposits on a multiple scale. (Board of Governors of the Federal Reserve System, 1963:72–74)

The reserve requirement is a powerful tool that the Fed can use for driving investment and trade or to contract the money supply so that the economy does not overheat. Because of its complicated nature, however, the reserve requirement has rarely made significant shifts. While the real effects of reserve banking have yet to be evaluated in a systematic study across international communities, reserve banking can be a powerful tool in the hands of those who have the knowledge and power to create or erase money.

The discount rate is another tool that the Federal Reserve uses to manage the economy. This is the interest rate that the various Federal Reserve banks charge lending institutions to borrow from them. The discount rate is "set by the Board of Directors of each of the Federal Reserve Banks, subject to approval by the Board of Governors" (Federal Reserve Bank of San Francisco, 1996a). This rate affects the rate at which these lending institutions can then lend money to businesses or consumers, having a lasting effect on the entire economy.

The final tool the Federal Reserve can use to manipulate the economy is its open market operations. This is the tool used most frequently. The Fed's open market operations are conducted through the buying and selling of government securities. The Federal Open Market Committee (FOMC) is the committee that controls this important monetary policy tool.

The FOMC is a twelve-member committee made up of the seven members of the Board of Governors; the president of the Federal Reserve Bank of New York; and, on a rotating basis, the presidents of four other Reserve Banks. It meets eight times a year to set Federal Reserve guidelines regarding the purchase and sale of government securities in the open market as a means of influencing the volume of bank credit and money in the economy. It also establishes policy relating to system operations in the foreign exchange markets. (Federal Reserve Board of Governors, September 27, 1996)

If the Federal Reserve makes the decision to release more liquidity into the market, it would need to buy back the government securities on the Open Market, hence increasing the money supply in the economy. The FOMC operates through the trading desk at the Federal Reserve Bank of New York by dictating the volume of securities to be purchased or sold on the open market.

The Fed pays for these securities by crediting the reserve accounts of banks involved with the sale. With more money in their reserve accounts, banks have more money to lend, and interest rates may decline. To tighten the money supply, the Fed sells government securities and collects payments from banks by reducing their reserve accounts. With less money in their reserve accounts, banks have less money to lend and interest rates may increase. (Federal Reserve Bank of San Francisco, 1996a)

The Federal Reserve has sought to control inflation since the early 1980s, thus squeezing the money supply and creating a strong dollar. Ronald Reagan fought and overcame inflation. Former Presidents Bush and Clinton kept a tight leash on inflation, thus driving the value of the dollar increasingly higher and causing exports to decrease due to higher prices abroad (see Exhibit 2 in Appendix A).

In 2001, interest rates were reduced to their lowest point in decades and massive amounts of liquidity were released into the markets, due to the weakening economy, to offset the negative economic impacts of the terrorist attacks on September 11, 2001. However, even the release of liquidity at record levels did not affect the value of the dollar much due to the fact that the rest of the world was feeling the effects of a global economic slowdown at the same time. Much of the world, like Japan for instance, was in even worse economic shape than the United States, so the dollar continued to be an attractive safety net for foreign investors.

Why should an administration risk political fallout when foreign markets are successfully financing U.S. deficits? The answer is two-fold. First, the foreign ownership of the U.S. debt (see Exhibit 3 in Appendix A) may cause the United States to compromise its policies in other arenas, such as foreign policy, due to its dependence on foreign financing. Not only is the United States dependent on international financing to sustain its standard-of-living level (see Exhibit 4 in Appendix A), but foreigners now hold large asset portfolios in the United States, far exceeding U.S. holdings abroad, which has a tremendous influence on the U.S. economy. Second, we have seen frightening examples of what has happened to countries with large trade deficits in the past. Throughout the 1970s and 1980s Latin American trade deficits were financed almost completely by foreign investors, just as the U.S. deficit is now. Studies have shown that

as late as 1981 the consensus was that Latin America could continue to borrow extensively for years to come. Yet in less than a year there was a collapse of financing that forced Latin America economies to cut imports by as much as two-thirds, plunging the region into a deep slump from which it still has not fully emerged. (Krugman, 1995:112–113)

It is unlikely that the damage to the United States would be as severe as it was in Latin America; however, the cost of losing foreign financial support would be staggering. "Our payments to foreigners are a direct drain on our resources, and the longer the trade deficits continue, the larger this drain will become" (Krugman, 1995:49).

Finally, policy makers, and particularly presidents, would face less political fallout if the Federal Reserve was preserved as an autonomous institution with a mandate to create trade policy that would effectively stimulate a balance of trade. Markets experience corrections sooner or later, as the United States witnessed in the early years of the 2000s after experiencing record growth in the late 1990s, and those corrections will be sharper and more prolonged if the market corrects itself without the Federal Reserve's intervention. Merely cutting the federal funds rate will not boost long-term confidence in the economy, as actions by the Japanese central bank and the U.S. Federal Reserve in 2001 demonstrated. If the Fed is not given the mandate, then the blame will be shouldered by the president alone.

Politically speaking, driving the value of the dollar down may actually be a favorable risk. Protectionists will likely continue to promote anti–free-trade themes in the future. Members on both sides of the political aisle will buy into these scare tactics which could severely damage any administration's drive to uphold free trade agreements such as NAFTA. By closing the trade deficit gap, protectionist ideologies may be curbed, thus allowing an administration to pursue other trade policy agendas.

IF NOT IN THE NATIONAL INTEREST, THEN IN WHOSE INTEREST IS A STRONG DOLLAR?

During the 1940s and 1950s the Federal Reserve noticed the importance of keeping trade deficits minimized, if for nothing else than the negative perception that a trade deficit might give to investors. In its own publication which outlined the purposes and functions of the Federal Reserve System fifty years after its creation, it states:

Loss of confidence in the dollar might even be generated through a build-up of speculative fears far in advance of real dangers, if people did not see progress toward elimination of the deficit. . . . It is therefore important to bring about adjustments in the U.S. balance of payments. . . . The emergence in recent years of large and continuous deficits in the U.S. balance of payments reflects in part the improved competitive position of foreign industrial countries in world trade. . . . During most of the time since the Federal Reserve System was established, balance of payments considerations have entered little into the making of monetary policy. But beginning in 1958, there emerged a large and persistent deficit in the payments balance. In such a situation the Federal Reserve has to take closely into account the effects of monetary policy on the balance of payments. (Board of Governors of the Federal Reserve System, 1963:156–158)

The Federal Reserve recognized the need, albeit grudgingly, to examine the effects of monetary policy on the balance of payments in 1963 when that publication was released. Why has it abandoned this view in more recent years?

The answer may very well lie with the Fed's dealings in the largest market in the world, the foreign exchange market, where currencies are bought and sold on a global scale. Over a trillion dollars is traded every day on this market.

The key here is that only an elite group of financial experts gets to play in this market, including bankers, brokers, large corporations, and central banks. Banks are by far the largest participants in the foreign exchange market. "They earn profits by buying currencies from, and selling currencies to, customers and to each other. Roughly two-thirds of FX [foreign exchange] transactions involve banks dealing directly with each other" (Gonnelli, 1993:29). These financial experts buy and sell currencies just like individuals buy and sell shares on the stock market.

The dollar is the currency most often used in the world's ongoing transactions, even if the United States is in no way involved in the transfer of goods or services. For example, if a transaction occurs between Saudi Arabia and Canada, they probably will use U.S. dollars to complete the transaction (Gonnelli, 1993:28–29). This fact alone demonstrates how the Federal Reserve System of the United States exerts international influence on the economies and policies of nation-states by actions it takes at home—an example of a powerful institution's constraining power and the growing interdependency that globalization is making a reality.

The dollar is used in international transactions because of the confidence that international investors have in it, a major reason why the Federal Reserve and the banking industry want to keep the dollar strong. As long as its value remains high, nations and individuals will continue to use the dollar, thus ensuring healthy profits for the banking industry which supplies the means of doing business. Banks and financiers who invest in the foreign exchange market bank on the fact that the dollar will remain strong against other currencies as the demand for the dollar remains strong. Slight movements in the exchange rate can mean a difference of millions of dollars.

It is in the best interests of the U.S. banking and financial sector, at least in the short run, to keep the value high so that global market transactions continue to occur in dollars. A strong dollar, however, automatically leads to an increase in the trade deficit as the cost of goods produced in the United States rises due to the high value of the dollar. This is the reason trade deficit management has been abandoned. The problem is, of course, the trade deficit will eventually cause investors to lose confidence in the dollar anyway. Therefore, long-term national interest is being pushed aside in favor of short-term profits.

THE TRADE DEFICIT SOLUTION

In the mid-1990s, Paul Krugman indicated that the dollar would have to be driven down about 20 to 25 percent from its level at that time to erase the trade deficit (Krugman, 1995:120). Federal Reserve Chairman Alan Greenspan is known for being conservative, and the Fed has been loathe to let the dollar fall. It is unlikely that the Fed would allow the value of the dollar to plunge as much as 20 to 25 percent, but the strategy of devaluation could be employed on a lesser scale, allowing the Federal Reserve to monitor the effects of the devaluation on the economy on a smaller scale while slowly closing the trade gap. Such a decrease in value will slow the growth of short-term U.S. wages, but it may increase the number of domestic jobs and will increase the consumption of domestically produced goods and increase long-term wage scales.

The Joint Economic Committee of the U.S. Congress performed a study of the economic impact of foreign trade deficits in 1984. The report stated:

The U.S. foreign sector will not show improvement . . . unless the deficit-bloated dollar shrinks substantially. . . . Underlying the sharp decline in the U.S. trade position is the striking price disadvantage confronting U.S. exporters. . . . Since 1979, for example, U.S. electrical machinery exports have risen 26 percent in price against competing Japanese and German products. The price of non-electrical U.S. machinery exports has jumped 33 percent, and U.S. transport equipment export prices are up 39 percent. As prices rose, export sales dropped. Between 1981 and 1984, for example, U.S. exports fell 13 percent or $37 billion. (Subcommittee on Economic Goals and Intergovernmental Policy of the Joint Economic Committee, 1984:10)

How far have we advanced since the 1984 report? The years immediately following the report proved to be the worst deficits in U.S. history, and in recent years the numbers have gotten even worse.

If a stronger currency decreases the price of imported goods relative to exported goods, then an appreciated dollar is one of the key factors contributing to the trade deficit. Therefore, the Federal Reserve's current policy perpetuates these deficits and renders the United States more dependent on foreign investors to finance them. This dependence is a grave national concern because it makes the United States dependent on foreign investment to sustain its standard-of-living level.

The psychological fear that this foreign dependence has cultivated is obvious in the growing number of protectionists. A protectionist ideology places an obstacle in the path of any administration's move towards free trade and feeds the movement towards isolationism. Isolationism is indeed a perilous maneuver because an already foreign-dependent trade deficit will completely collapse if tighter tariff controls are instigated due to isolationist policies. When the Bush administration raised tariffs on steel imports in 2002, the European Union and Russia quickly countered by raising tariffs on U.S. goods. Tariffs often hurt domestic manufacturers that depend on cheaper raw materials and generally have the additional side effect of souring relations between trading nations. A collapse of the U.S. trade market would handicap the entire economy and would curtail U.S. influence in global economic policy making. Many policy analysts argue that U.S. status has already been severely undermined due to its growing trade deficit, but its attractiveness to foreign investors has kept it the viable actor in the international arena that it still is today.

A country cannot continue to finance a perpetually increasing debt. A continuation of current policies will eventually force the market to correct itself through a massive uncontrolled devaluation of the dollar, which would have devastating effects on the U.S. economy and cause unemployment rates to skyrocket. In September of 1999 the *New York Times* reported that the U.S. trade deficit figures were at the very root of the recent plunges taken by the Dow Jones industrial average as Wall Street recognized the perceived threat to the dollar due to the U.S. trade deficit rising at an alarming rate (Sanger, 1999).

More money is sent abroad each and every year to pay off the foreign financing of the U.S. deficits. This is money that is lost elsewhere, that cannot be reinvested into the economy to boost productivity levels and allow wages to grow at faster rates than inflation.

Stagnant productivity levels in the United States in the early 1990s along with a booming U.S. economy, amid global financial crises elsewhere in the latter 1990s, have caused the trade deficit gap to increase. The lower productivity levels in the early 1990s led to a lower quality of goods and services while causing prices to inflate, and the global crisis of the late 1990s led to an increase in international investment in the dollar as foreign economies faltered. Meanwhile new wealth, or the perception of wealth, caused U.S. consumers to buy up imported goods in vast amounts.

Many economists and policy experts have been slow to criticize the trade deficit because exports comprise a very small portion of U.S. GDP, generally between 10 and 15 percent. However, jobs that stem from international exports are higher paying than average domestic jobs, and exports actually formulate a substantial portion of economic growth, measured in value, in the United States even though they represent a small percentage of the economy as a whole.

The increasing trade deficit is a paramount national security concern. OECD countries are buying up U.S. assets and are financing its trade deficit with capital and financial investments. Not only does the United States count on foreign investment for its sustained standard of living, but foreign ownership compromises the sovereignty of the United States. "The trade deficit and the growing foreign stake [in the U.S.] tend to feed crude forms of economic nationalism at home, increasing the risks of a trade war" (Krugman, 1995: 50).

The United States cannot afford to continue to mortgage its deficits to foreign investors and expect to maintain its current standard-of-living level. As foreigners increase their U.S. asset portfolios, foreign governments will have more power to wield ideological and economic influence in domestic and international policy because the United States may have to compromise with other nations in order to sustain its economic viability. Or, even more likely, as the U.S. trade deficit begins to concern international investors, they may sell their dollars and invest them elsewhere, causing inflationary forces to set in which decrease asset values, thus lowering or slowing the growth of the standard-of-living level.

Decreasing the value of the dollar on the international exchange rate system is one viable policy the government can implement to erase this peril without making changes in the budget. Prior to September 11, 2001, Congress had figured out a way to eliminate chronic budget deficits,[16] and in the absence of budget deficits a devaluation of the dollar is more effective at erasing trade deficits.

A devaluation in the dollar will slow the wage growth of Americans (which will indirectly slow the rate of import consumption) while decreasing U.S. prices will be attractive to foreign markets (which will increase U.S. exports). Initially, the phenomenon known as the J-curve will take place (see Exhibit 5 in Appendix A). When the currency is first devalued,

> trade balance worsens as the cost of previously ordered exports remains unchanged. [The] trade balance begins to improve as the lower cost of exports stimulates foreign demand and the relatively high price of imports depresses demand for them. (Gonnelli, 1993:31)

The bottom line is this: cheaper dollars create cheaper American goods on foreign markets. In turn, this price decrease will promote a proportional increase in foreign demand and result in higher export productivity.

The political risk of devaluing the dollar is ominous but could be lessened by giving the Federal Reserve the mandate to promote a balance of trade. The Fed could then create policy that would benefit the country as a whole. While certain industries that depend on foreign imports may suffer initially, such as the automobile dealerships, other markets will improve, such as domestic automobile manufacturers. Long-term wages will increase along with aggregate domestic employment rates and job growth. These positive factors will reduce protectionist movements allowing free trade policies to move forward and sustaining U.S. economic importance in the international community.

As a top-echelon player in an interdependent global economy, the United States will be able to continue to wield influence in other areas of concern to its national security by using its economic might as leverage instead of merely playing its military prowess trump card. When economic prowess is well known, economic sanctions may be just as effective in certain foreign policy situations as bombs and ground troops; however, the method is much more humane. There will always be a need for a national defense, and there will most certainly be times when dropping bombs is necessary, such as in rooting out terrorist cells in Afghanistan, but economics can be a very powerful tool in specific situations.

Meanwhile, as J. A. Hobson's (1965) underconsumption theory would indicate higher paying jobs at home would allow for higher levels of domestic consumption while lower export prices on U.S.

goods would increase domestic output, therefore allowing productivity levels and standard-of-living levels to rise without having to resort to imperialistic or mercantile policies abroad.

THE GERMAN EXPERIENCE

The Germans have attempted to enforce conservative monetary policies ever since their experiences in mismanagement of the economy in the Weimar era. As the member countries of the European Monetary Union have moved toward a single European currency, the euro, many German citizens and policy makers have become understandably concerned with the real possibility of losing control over that economic stability. It is still too early to tell how the member states will react to the varying ideological and philosophical management styles, but it is certainly quite feasible that friction will occur as countries ultimately give up a great deal of sovereignty when dealing with monetary policy and have to deal with the effects of other countries' budgetary problems.

Germany's central bank, the Bundesbank, has been quite successful in the past in not only constraining domestic policy choices but also at shaping EU policies. The Bundesbank has done this by convincing other member states to comply with Bundesbank demands on the structure of the European Monetary System (EMS) by threatening to pull financial support. Karl Kaltenthaler (1998) describes how domestic institutions gave a vehicle to the interested actors involved, particularly the German banking industry, and how these institutions shaped the resulting system that has emerged.

Concerns about the future distributional consequences of the EMS in Germany were the primary motivations for both state and societal organizations' behavior in the debate over the initiation of the regime and the conflict over its design. While the distributional consequences of the EMS drove the motivations of the actors in Germany who hoped to shape policy toward the monetary regime, it was how domestic policy institutions shaped the conflict between the interested organizations that determined the dynamics of Germany policy. How institutions divide the responsibility for policy among state organizations and how they give societal actors a say in the policy process clearly mattered to how the German government decided on the rules of the EMS. (Kaltenthaler, 1998:55)

Germany has placed a great deal of importance on global trade. It ran annual surpluses throughout most of the 1990s, in spite of the reunification process with East Germany. This result was not pure coincidence but an intended policy result. A German embassy brief released on the economic structure of the nation stated, "The goal is to ensure price stability, high employment levels and a stable trade balance while maintaining steady and adequate economic growth" (U.S. Department of State, September 1996).

The Bundesbank demonstrated its commitment to maintaining a positive trade balance by keeping tight controls over the value of the deutsche mark. An example of this is when the dollar was temporarily undermined by the crisis in Mexico at the end of 1994 amid pervasive economic turmoil throughout Europe. The Bundesbank witnessed a massive increase in deutsche mark investment as countries began pouring their funds into deutsche marks instead of dollars. The Bundesbank quickly took action in 1995 by easing back on their monetary policy to provide for a devaluation of the currency (U.S. Treasury, January 15, 1996). The move slowed the economic growth rate, and the tightening of the money supply had some lingering effects in regard to an increase in the unemployment rate, but the rate of inflation still remained far below the German target parameters of 2 percent (U.S. Treasury, January 15, 1996).

TRADE POLICY: INTEREST RATE MANAGEMENT AND THE DEFICIT

Once European integration begins to smooth out the rough edges, the already powerful trading bloc, including three of the five largest economies in the world (Germany, France, and the United Kingdom), will become far more powerful in regards to setting the agenda for international policy issues, trade, and even defense, as the European Union begins to wield more economic might in its status as an integrated body of nations.

It has been the policy of the U.S. Federal Reserve, and every administration since Ronald Reagan, to concentrate almost wholly on inflation without regard to trade. In March 1996 Alan Greenspan reiterated his past policy moves before the Senate Banking Committee hearing on his renomination, stating that "monetary policy's foremost goal should be suppression of inflation because price stability is a fundamental condition for the U.S. economy to reach its potential" (Rose, 1996:1). These inflation-fighting policies, however, have the lasting effect of keeping the value of the dollar at a very high level because the Fed keeps a tight hold on the money supply through high interest rates. The dollar is worth more because there are fewer of them in circulation. The United States has enjoyed the prestige of a strong dollar because it attracts foreign investment. The negative side effect of a strong dollar is that it frustrates exportation. Policy makers in the United States have not been alarmed with trade deficits in the past because only about 10 percent of the economy depended on trade. Each year, however, trade has grown more important. Every year that the United States sustains a trade deficit, it grows increasingly more dependent on foreign investment to sustain its standard of living.

Germany demonstrated that a country need not give up its inflation-fighting policies to achieve a trade balance. A healthy economy is in the national interest, and the size of the U.S. economy requires a partnership between the private and public sectors. From the public side, the Federal Reserve should pursue trade policy which focuses on a balance of trade and interest rate management. The Federal Reserve has taken on a more active role in the economy in the past. Marriner Eccles, the former Fed chief whose name adorns the Board of Governor's building in Washington, D.C., was known to be a progressive banker with Keynesian ideas about the U.S. economy, so it is not outside the realm for the Fed to play a larger role outside its present management style. Congress, correspondingly, needs to continue to make the tough decisions to strive for a balanced budget when feasible. There are times when deficit spending is both prudent and necessary, and there are times when it merely crowds out investment.

If the trade deficit was brought under control, the pressure that the United States has witnessed to maintain the high value of the dollar so as to attract foreign investment to finance the deficit causing negative savings rates in the past would theoretically be lessened. The demand for foreign financing to sustain an acceptable standard of living should be lessened as well, thus allowing the dollar to be devalued so as to help achieve real, long-term productivity rates. Not only will the trade deficit gap be closed, due to the depreciation of the dollar, but future foreign pressure on American policy makers will be reduced as interdependent global traders theoretically grow increasingly dependent on U.S. exports to sustain their standard-of-living levels.

It is evident that while balancing the federal budget is important to economic policy and helps in bringing down the overall current account deficit, reducing the budget deficit is not enough by itself to heavily impact the current account deficit. As mentioned earlier, the trade deficit is the largest driver of the current account deficit. The U.S. current account deficit for 1994 was about 2.2 percent of GDP, and about 2.1 percent of GDP for 1995. This decline had a positive correlation with the Clinton administration's successful attempt at slowing the growth of the deficit. Experts forecasted a continuing decline in the current account deficit to approximately 1.75 percent of GDP if the Clinton administration held firmly to its campaign promise that the budget would be balanced within seven years. The promise was kept, but the correlation did not hold true. Current account deficits have actually increased as a percent of GDP in recent years, reflecting the impact of trade deficits more than budget surpluses.

Deficits do hinder productivity growth. Basic macroeconomic theory would dictate that if a nation can get its productivity to rise faster than its rate of inflation, then wages can still rise while the prices of products remain at their current levels. This would indicate an economy was growing at a positive rate and that a wage-earner's dollar would go farther in the marketplace. Productivity has not always grown faster than inflation in the United States, however, and therefore the Federal Reserve has generally tried to achieve the solution to the aforementioned equation by strangling inflation.

Of course, any country would like to boost its productivity levels while maintaining control over excessive inflation; this is the best scenario. Doing so permits the country to keep unemployment levels down while allowing wages to increase. The relationship between unemployment and inflation is typically inverse. For example, if a country is struggling with a high rate of inflation and its leaders want to bring that rate down, the standard policy would be to strangle the economy by raising interest rates and pulling money out of circulation. This type of action would usually increase the unemployment rate.

In order to reach full employment and full productivity, it is necessary to create a surge in demand, thus creating a catalyst to drive the economy. Devaluing the U.S. dollar would create this surge in demand in the United States. Now, if demand explodes to a level that exceeds the capacity of the economy, inflation sets in. This phenomenon is precisely why the budget must be kept in balance, so that the percentage of GDP that would normally have to finance the deficit, and therefore cut into U.S. savings, can be reinvested into the economy, helping keep supply in balance with the growing demand (Woodrow: Federal Reserve Bank of Minneapolis, February 20, 1996).

THE BUNDESBANK

The Bundesbank is Germany's central banking institution that was responsible for creating monetary policy for the German economy prior to the country's monetary integration with other EU member states. It is important to note that the Bundesbank has not disappeared. Rather, it serves as a national branch within more of a regional context within the European System of Central Banks. The Bundesbank was legendary for its conservative inflation-fighting strategy. During its prime years as the all-powerful central bank of Germany, it concentrated on the stabilization, issuance, and guarantee of deutsche mark notes (DM).

The Bundesbank was even more autonomous than the U.S. Federal Reserve and had almost no governmental interference in policy. Bundesbank officials are appointed for eight-year terms. Top officials are nominated by the government "and the president appoints, and there is no official requirement for parliamentary consultation" (Sbragia and Woolley, 1992:177).

The Bundesbank controlled monetary policy much in the same way as the U.S. Federal Reserve. The Bundesbank Council, which served in a capacity similar to the Federal Open Market Committee in the U.S. Federal Reserve System, was in charge of creating monetary policy. Members of the Bundesbank Council include "the eleven presidents of the land central banks and the seven members of the Bundesbank directorate" (Sbragia and Woolley, 1992:176). The tools that the Bundesbank used to conduct monetary policy were similar to the U.S. Federal Reserve's tools. The main tools were:

1. Establishing and monitoring the monetary target range, which defines how much and fast certain quantities of the money supply are expected

to grow. This is usually done by tracking broad money, or M3, which the Bundesbank has established is the "broadest measure of [the] money supply:[it] includes currency in circulation, sight deposits, time deposits of under 4 years, and saving deposits at 3 months' notice";

2. The Lombard rate and the discount rate, which are the rates at which commercial banks can borrow from the Bundesbank; and

3. The repo rate, the rate at which securities are repurchased by the Bundesbank. (German News Team, October 1996)

The council, known as the *Zentralbankrat*, meets each week on Thursday and handles all major policy decisions. The branch banks are representative of each German state, known as *Landesbanken*. Through these banking institutions, the Bundesbank controls the commercial banking industry and the flow of currency into the German economy.

Once the European Exchange Rate Mechanism (ERM) was established, the Bundesbank took on the role of intervenor, meaning that the Bundesbank was obligated to intervene when a participating nation-state's currency fell below the predetermined level of acceptance, which basically meant that the Bundesbank was acting as the central bank for the participating states until the European Central Bank was formally established.

Now that several members of the EU have moved toward complete economic integration, it is helpful to understand some of the most important terminology. The European Economic and Monetary Union (EMU) obligates all EMU participants within the EU "to adopt a common monetary policy, link their currencies firmly together and harmonize their economic policies" (Lanjouw, 1995:86).

The European currency unit (ECU) was the "European unit of account, reserve asset and numeraire based on a basket of EU currencies weighted according to economic importance" (Lanjouw, 1995:86), which was the unit being used to establish the benchmark for the European Monetary System (EMS) to set the value of the euro.

The EMS is "a framework established by the EU countries to promote exchange rate stability in Europe" (Lanjouw, 1995:87). This rate is currently established through the ERM and will continue to be the exchange rate regulator for other EU countries that do not convert to the euro.

The ERM is a regulating mechanism that functions on the "basis of fixed but adjustable parities. The participating exchange rates are kept within set limits, with an obligation to intervene if the rate threatens to exceed those limits" (Lanjouw, 1995:88). The ERM has fluctuated from plus or minus 15 percent around the ECU to plus or minus 2.25 percent. At times this obligation proved too strenuous for many member countries such as Italy and Great Britain which both tried desperately to hold their exchange rates at artificial levels until unemployment rates became politically infeasible and both countries had to pull out of the ERM. Italy did recuperate and met the Maastricht requirements in time to join the EMU in 1999. However, this is an example of a situation where Germany will be vulnerable in the new EMU, in that ultimately the responsibility to intervene may fall on Germany in cases where countries cannot afford to make extravagant payments into their own state coffers to adjust their exchange rates within the prescribed limits. Germany has been able to do this in the past, but at the cost of its own rising unemployment rate. Critics are uncertain whether Germany will be able to play such a role in the future, as its own political and economic struggles are increasingly being blamed on integration. Thus EMU and EU support is becoming less popular among many German citizens.

The strong deutsche mark established a solid reputation that sustained foreign investment in the mark. However, the euro has not yet achieved the same level of confidence. This could prove to have a disastrous effect on the EMS should any countries fall outside the ERM and need financial support.

The question now is whether Germany can continue to be successful in shaping EU economic policy as further integration persists. It would be extremely naive to believe that the Bundesbank will not continue to play a significant role in the new European System of Central Banks. In fact, the Bundesbank has already played a very significant role in the shape and structure of the new system, showing strong opposition to many of the European central bank's plans to conduct monetary policy by a direct inflation target approach, which targets price movements. Instead, the Bundesbank has been adamantly in favor of a strategy which concentrates on intermediate target variables to measure monetary growth. The Bundesbank's scientific reasoning for its support of this approach is that the transmission channel from the deployment of the monetary policy instruments up to the final objective of monetary policy needs to be sufficiently well-known and calculable . . . and experience has shown that inflation is always a monetary phenomenon, irrespective of the different factors which trigger price rises. (Deutsche Bundesbank, April 18, 1996:104–105)

The Bundesbank was not afraid to promote its approach further by boasting about its own past performance using the intermediate target strategy in the following statement, "Such intermediate targets have proved their worth in 20 years of use as the key target variable for monetary policy decisions in Germany" (Deutsche Bundesbank, April 18, 1996:105). The Bundesbank then inserted a promotional advertisement for the adoption of German policy influence by stating that "the adoption of such a strategy by the European System of Central Banks (ESCB) will require, however, that the links between the money stock and prices are similarly stable in the monetary union as they have been hitherto in Germany" (Deutsche Bundesbank, April 18, 1996:105). Germany's anti-inflationary policies will no doubt be more difficult to implement, however, as more countries are brought into the monetary mix, especially if and when their lesser-developed former Eastern bloc neighbors are brought into the monetary union.

The risk of a volatile common currency has left international investors somewhat apprehensive about investing in the euro. The European central bank does enjoy political autonomy similar to the Bundesbank, which Germany argues is important due to the conflicting ideologies of the member states. Although it is uncertain whether conservative inflation-controlling measures are likely to remain the main policy objectives for the new central bank, especially considering problems that some member countries have had in the past with their own currencies.

Germany under former Chancellor Kohl was the leader in pushing for fulfillment of the economic measures that were laid out in the Maastricht Treaty, hence moving toward completion of the EMU, and the single currency. There was a Stability Pact agreed to among the various ministers to force member states to maintain fiscal responsibility at home. The Pact included, among other things, an obligation by member states to keep their domestic budget deficit levels below a 3 percent GDP benchmark.

Germany, France, Italy, and many other nations found the 3 percent budget deficit level the most difficult criterion to meet for the 1999 target date. France actively engaged in transferring billions of francs from pension payments of state agencies into the state coffers in order to bring its deficit level into compliance. Germany made payments into its state treasury in an attempt to meet guidelines as well, causing inflation to rise at a higher than normal rate (Reuters World Service, September 27, 1996). Reacting sharply to criticism that the guidelines set out by Maastricht were perhaps too strict, German Chancellor Helmut Kohl responded in 1996, "The criteria and the deadline are not open to discussion. Any change could endanger the entire project" (Reuters Word Service, September 27, 1996). He was not ready to let wavering public support derail something he had spent his whole public career working to implement. Kohl also assured Germans that the European central bank would be fashioned after the German Bundesbank and that the common currency, the euro, would be as stable as the deutsche mark. Therefore, the short-term sacrifices of the German people would reap long-term benefits. Consequently, Germany moved forward with economic integration without Kohl at the helm, as the national sacrifices proved too much for the German public and they voted their long-time leader out of office.

In light of the research question addressed in this study, it is somewhat perplexing that Germany as a state put its national interest at risk. It is quite obvious that the banking and business sectors will benefit from the falling trade barriers and the removal of transaction costs that are associated with currency exchange, but Germany, as a nation-state, is risking its dominating role in Western Europe. The risk of falling to a "sideline" status rather than a "player" status is ominous. On the one hand, Germany stands to gain one common currency and unilateral policies within a large trading bloc, which will dramatically boost its trade income due to lowered barriers and the removal of massive inefficient bureaucratic bulwarks.

On the other hand, Germany risks losing its superpower trade status as the Bundesbank gives up its economic autonomy to a European central banking institution that Germany cannot singlehandedly control. Should the venture fail, the economies of the EU member states will suffer mightily, resulting in an economic recession which could possibly take decades to recover from. Once the movement toward economic integration began, however, it is quite possible that institutional constraints pushed Germany into giving up its power role as Western Europe's financial hegemon in order not to be left out of the new economic power bloc.

CONCLUSION

Neither the United States nor Germany need to consider drastic policy changes in order to merely survive; however, both are in situations in which policy initiatives could ultimately mold their long-term status in the global community. If the United States does nothing, it will surely require more foreign financing to subsidize the standard-of-living level until ultimately the market will correct itself by devaluing the dollar due to international investors' concerns over the massive trade deficit gap. Corrective measures could be taken now to devalue the dollar in small increments in order to close the deficit gap without long-lasting recessionary repercussions.

Germany could have continued its annual trade surpluses and remained in the political and economic policy "driver's seat" for the next decade while regional trade agreements grew up around it, or it might have risked its comfortable status for the possibility of long-term economic stability and productivity growth, albeit at the hands of supranational authority and economic interdependence. The former scenario is the path it has chosen, and only time will tell if it is the right path. Helmut Kohl will undoubtedly be remembered as the leader who championed one of the most massive economic and political transitions of all time due to the monetary integration of the EU, but will he also be remembered as the man who singlehandedly toppled Germany's superpower status? Either way, his zealous efforts to push through economic integration cost the long-time political veteran his job, as he lost the election in 1998 when economic pressures and increasing unemployment rates finally made German voters wary of the costs of unification and integration within the same decade.

The United States and Germany are two of the most instrumental players in the world's economy. Both countries have central banking institutions and policy makers that believe in rigid anti-inflationary monetary policies, and similarly, both countries have had currencies in the past decade that have been the envy of the other nation-states in the world. However, when comparing trade data, the congruencies between these two countries dissolve. Germany's central bank, an autonomous institution with a clear policy objective to engage in active trade policy, assisted the country in achieving annual trade surpluses. The U.S. Federal Reserve, on the other hand, with no clear trade policy objectives and its rigid efforts to maintain a strong dollar has unintentionally helped perpetuate the massive trade deficits in the United States.

In past decades U.S. policy makers did not concern themselves with the trade deficit because the vast majority of the nation's economic activity occurred within its own borders. Central bankers and banking industry lobbyists assured powerful policy makers that it was prestigious to have a strong dollar, spurring international financiers to seek out investment opportunities within the United States.

The question of why the Federal Reserve abandoned the idea of monitoring policy that caused trade imbalances has been answered at least in part by the fact that the foreign exchange market is making massive amounts of money for the financial sector as the high-valued dollar continues to be the currency of choice for international transactions, thus giving the financial lobby little reason to push an alternative policy. However, the economic activity of the United States and the rest of the world has taken on a new global flavor. The United States will have to remain competitive on a worldwide basis if it intends to sustain its standard-of-living level at home, not just with over-inflated equities and a budget surplus, but also with trade balances and increased consumption of domestically produced goods.

Trade will continually grow in importance and should not be left to fiscal policy alone. The U.S. Congress should consider giving the Federal Reserve a mandate to create trade policy which institutes a balance of trade. Congress has the authority to do this and has given mandates to the Federal Reserve in the past. Only then can the United States ensure that the Federal Reserve will engage in interest rate management practices that control the trade balance and not fall prey to outside political pressures which can hinder the nation's long-term economic outlook.

Germany has proven the prudence of its monetary and trade policies through decades of productivity growth, a stable economy, and annual trade surpluses. It will be interesting to see if it can take this success and use it as a catalyst for the emerging European Union and its system of central banks. The United States, on the other hand, needs to create policy which will institute a balance of trade so as to ensure its future economic prowess in the new global economy. Sagacious trade policies now can ease the country back into a healthy trade balance without the painful blows of a massive devaluation which will likely occur if the United States waits for the markets to return to historical averages.

Trade deficits in the United States are already concerning international investors as they worry about the true value of assets, worries that have been validated in part by the stock market which has fluctuated from explosive growth in the latter 1990s to collapsing prices in the early 2000s. A prolonged recession, the long-term mortgaging of assets to foreigners, or the complete sell-off of businesses and assets to foreign investors are not in the national interest. Such policy moves may benefit certain sectors of the society whose ideas become imbedded in institutions that constrain national policy, but any time national sovereignty or economic stability is called into question, the interests of the nation as a whole are not being looked after. When money leaves the United States, future investment is lost and productivity potential is lowered.

This chapter has demonstrated that trade deficits are not in the national interest; in fact, when trade deficits are sustained over long periods of time and allowed to spiral out of control, they are detrimental to the well-being of a nation.

It is apparent that the policies of the Federal Reserve System do not produce trivial domestic effects that have no real influence on the well-being of the nation-state or the international system. This finding is troubling for an all-encompassing systemic theory.

It is evident that institutions do matter in the United States, as this case study of the U.S. Federal Reserve System has shown; and similar studies of the German Bundesbank as an institution, as noted in this chapter, have demonstrated that it has been very influential in shaping and constraining domestic and regional policy as well. Institutions merely reflect the interests of certain actors, and the banking industry in the United States, along with the financial elite who needed the banking industry to thrive, have imbedded their interests in the powerful institution that acts as a constraining economic and monetary policy force for the United States and the world, the U.S. Federal Reserve System.

Chapter 6

Final Thoughts

International trade is a topic that headlines newspapers and television news journals, is used as a buzzword in boardrooms around the globe, and is talked about in classrooms and in passing social conversation, but what does it really mean in terms of the national interest? In many export-dominated countries, it means the health of those nations' economies. In other countries where trade has traditionally played a smaller role, international trade can mean sustaining a certain standard-of-living level, but it may not be essential for survival. The United States belongs to the latter group, though the trend is rapidly changing.

In the industrialized and postindustrialized world, banking drives trade and investment. In the United States in particular, the monetary policies being implemented cause trade deficits; therefore, in essence, the banking policy of the United States is its trade policy. This statement is not referring to bilateral trade agreements that the president of the United States negotiates and Congress later ratifies or the political debates over which countries get Most Favored Nation (MFN) status. It concerns how the real moneymakers constrain policy to get rich from foreign exchange markets by keeping the dollar strong while abandoning any policy that works toward a trade balance.

A weaker dollar, which may actually more accurately represent the real value of the dollar and which is needed to bring the U.S. trade deficit under control, means less profit for the financial sector.

This fact alone means that the dollar will not see a prescribed devaluation anytime soon, even if it is in the national interest to bring the trade deficit under control. That is why the issue of trade deficits in the United States had to be studied from the banking angle—U.S. banking policy is its macro-trade policy.

In the new age of electronic commerce when finance capital can be moved in fractions of a second, central banks have come under some new constraints whereby their regulatory powers may have little effect. Financiers can take out loans from banks to buy large quantities of a nation's currency, driving the price of that currency up. Once the currency price has been driven up, these financiers can sell off the currency in hordes, making huge profits and ultimately undermining the value of the currency. The entire financial system of a country may collapse, sending shock waves through the entire international economic system due to increasing interdependency. Gregory J. Millman explained that this is how George Soros' hedge fund caused Great Britain and Italy to pull out of the European ERM in the early 1990s (Millman, 1995:58–64).

Hedge funds have grown in purchasing power and in number.

There may be over a thousand hedge funds. No one is sure of the exact number, because they are not regulated. At least a dozen hedge fund managers, like Soros, manage more than $1 billion each. Many of them trade currencies, and made handsome profits when the EMS [European Monetary System] went down, but only George Soros was willing to be publicly identified as the nemesis of the central banks and the guru of international finance. The others would rather not be noticed. (Millman, 1995:60)

However, what may be even more frightening than a bunch of renegade capitalists running around unregulated trying to make profits at the expense of national economies is that in the developing world there is evidence that central banks, the so-called national agents of international economic stability, are out there doing the same thing. The central bank of Malaysia is an example of one central bank that engages in such practices for its own profit. In the mid-1980s, Malaysia's central bank started its rogue financial behavior in retaliation for a G-5 action which severely decreased the country's purchasing power (Millman, 1995:225–229).

Using all the resources a central bank commands—privileged information, unlimited credit, regulatory power, and more—Malaysia's Bank Negara became the most feared trader in the currency markets. By trading for profit, Bank Negara committed apostasy against the creed of central banking. Instead of working to ensure global financial stability, Bank Negara repeatedly shoved huge sums of money into the most vulnerable market situations in order to destabilize exchange rates for its own profit. (Millman, 1995:226)

There were two models in international relations theory—institutional and neorealist—that were looked at in this study. The neorealist model dominates the field and is used in deciding most foreign policy. The largest fault with this model is its unit of analysis, the nation-state. While nation-states certainly are important actors in the international system, countries are not the only influential actors in international relations. The neorealist model relies on the fact that domestic institutions work toward the national interest, or else are too trivial to have an impact on the national interest, and that international organizations are inconsequential to the systemic balance of power.

The institutional model supports the idea that institutions, both domestic and international, do matter and can constrain the actions of nation-states. Robert O. Keohane, Joseph S. Nye, and Stanley Hoffmann lay out one of the most fundamental and important distinctions between institutionalist theory and neorealist theory in the introduction to *After the Cold War: International Institutions and State Strategies in Europe, 1989–1991*. They state that "the rules of institutions constrain the bargaining strategies of states and therefore make their actions more predictable" (Keohane, Nye, and Hoffman, 1993:15). They go on to say that "institutions seem to have affected how governments view their own interests: that is, institutionalization can affect *preferences*" (Keohane et al., 1993:15–16).

The financial sector—with its interests imbedded in a domestic institution, the Federal Reserve System—has affected U.S. policy through selecting preferences and agenda-setting, leading it down the dangerous path of compounding trade deficits while having international influence on how the entire world does business. The pressure by the financial sector to keep the dollar strong has changed the world economy, but at what cost?

Keeping the dollar high to appease consumers of imported products and corporations that depend on cheap labor abroad while guaranteeing the continued use of the dollar as the currency of choice in international transactions is not the best long-term national strategy. It looks great on the surface, but further analysis demonstrates that there are definite winners and losers in this scenario. Many have argued that other sectors, particularly the manufacturing sector, have been sold out by the financial sector. A lobbyist from the manufacturing sector explained to William Greider:

We still think of manufacturing as the "big mule" in politics, but it's not true. The financial sector, the retailing sector, the service sector are all so much bigger. The strong dollar was good for them and it was good for consumers. (Greider, 1987:600)

The benefits are certainly politically appealing, but they are also short-term, as deficits erode investor confidence and lead to inevitable uncontrolled corrections in currency values.

The world witnessed a global economic crisis in 1998 when the Federal Reserve was forced to bail out a hedge fund for capitalizing on a system that its own industry had created. Countries which had nothing to do with the investments of LTCM were forced to pay the consequences of a small group of capitalists, some of whom were former executives in the Federal Reserve System, looking to get richer while currency values and entire banking systems of countries which were paying back loans in a timely fashion collapsed because of a risky venture gone awry. The Federal Reserve bailed out the fund and took over the claims, staving off a global meltdown. This is an example that demonstrates how the actions of the Federal Reserve, domestically and internationally, cannot be seen as inconsequential.

Institutions are not mere anomalies that *exist* in nation-states or in the international system, but instead are often constraining forces of policy. There is no doubt that institutions can and do play a major role in promoting the interests of nation-states. The Federal Reserve has definitely had its moments when it acted as an agent on behalf of the national interest. Marriner Eccles, whose bold and brilliant policies helped bring the United States out of the Great Depression, was indeed a central banker who worked hard to promote the national interest. Alan Greenspan, economist turned pop culture legend, demonstrated the Fed's ability and willingness to be a major tool in promoting the national interest when the Fed pulled the banking system together in the wake of the largest terrorist attack ever committed on American soil on September 11, 2001, and flooded the markets with liquidity to keep the wheels of the economy churning. But to argue that institutions are merely tools of the state that exist without regard for their own interests, or the interests of other sectors of society, or that the actions of institutions are irrelevant in how nation-states behave in the international system altogether, is to miss an increasingly more important piece of the global systemic puzzle.

Institutions can and should play a major role in setting an agenda in which community leaders get together and create policy toward the long-term national interest, or international community interest, depending on whether the institution is domestic or international in scope. If institutions refuse to do it on their own, then legislative bodies, whether domestic or international, must take back control and instigate mandates that more closely regulate the functions of these institutions, making them more transparent so that goals, missions, and policies can be effectively measured and evaluated. There has been some discussion of doing this in the highly unregulated arena of financial investment, though the lobby against such measures will be awesome. John H. Jackson notes in his book *The World Trading System: Law and Policy of International Economic Relations* that some policy makers have been trying to work out agreements on international investment and capital flows that coincide with current trade agreements regulated by the WTO.

In many ways, the link between trade and investment is so intimate that it would be difficult to see how the investment subjects can be kept out of the WTO. Thus it is not entirely surprising that a strong push has been made to develop new international cooperative legal norms relating to investment and capital flows. Some of this has been developed in the context of the OECD; others propose, however, that the matter be taken up directly in the WTO. (Jackson, 1999:245)

If scholars, policy makers, business leaders, labor representatives, institutions, and practitioners can all come together and work on setting the policy agenda in the true national interest whereby the entire nation prospers over a sustained period while keeping the balance of payments in check, all segments and sectors of society can see an increase in the standard-of-living level without mortgaging economic prosperity or national security to foreign investors whose interests are personal, short term, and unmotivated by the interests of the country being invested in or the citizens who live and work there.

Not only will this type of cooperation raise the standard-of-living level for the majority of the populace within the home state, but it will also decrease the likelihood of foreign speculation, and imperialistic tendencies, as powerful industries and institutions focus on domestic investment and consumption rather than securing foreign markets or special economic zones abroad for fostering cheap labor.

This type of cooperation can lead to long-term economic prosperity, rather than economic swings and upheavals, and may also promote better international relations as countries feel less threatened from speculative foreign investors. Such cooperation is in the spirit of the institutional model.

If this type of cooperation is not achieved, the world can expect a frightening scenario as markets plunge due to inevitable corrections when investors pull capital from markets they determine to be unworthy of their time and money, not unlike William Greider's doomsday account of the modern global economy in his book, *One World, Ready or Not: The Manic Logic of Global Capitalism.*

Financial investors monitor and punish corporations or whole industrial sectors if their returns weaken. Finance disciplines governments or even entire regions of the globe if those places appear to be creating impediments to profitable enterprise or unpleasant surprises for capital. If this sounds dictatorial, the global financiers also adhere to their own rough version of egalitarian values: they will turn on anyone, even their own home country's industry and government, if the defense of free capital seems to require it. (Greider, 1997:25)

Those who believe that the pursuit of money and profits is not a powerful mechanism that can bring governments to their knees should heed the words of Gregory Millman.

[Now] it is the banks, investment banks, hedge funds, and other private financial institutions that judge governments and punish them financially. Their vigilante economics acknowledges no national border, bows to no regulatory authority, accepts no rule but the rule of financial power, and enforces rough justice against those who violate the law of the market. (Millman, 1995:98)

Policy makers must acknowledge the power of finance capital, embrace the possibilities it creates under a well-managed, transparent banking system, and fear its implications in the new global economy if it continues to go underregulated. I do believe, however, that cooperation, through participation by the world's financial institutions, legislative bodies, nation-states, policy makers, and scholars can create a structure that benefits the entire international system while raising the standard-of-living levels of the citizens of the nations they regulate.

Appendix A

Exhibits

Exhibit 1
Multiplying Capacity of Reserve Money through Bank Transactions (in dollars)

Transactions	Deposited in Checking Accounts	Lent	Set Aside as Reserves
Bank 1	100.00	80.00	20.00
Bank 2	80.00	64.00	16.00
Bank 3	64.00	51.20	12.80
Bank 4	51.20	40.96	10.24
Bank 5	40.96	32.77	8.19
Bank 6	32.77	26.22	6.55
Bank 7	26.22	20.98	5.24
Bank 8	20.98	16.78	4.20
Bank 9	16.78	13.42	3.36
Bank 10	13.42	10.74	2.68
Total for 10 Banks	446.33	357.07	89.26
Additional Banks (adjusted to offset rounding in preceding figures)	53.67	42.93	10.74
Grand Total of All Banks	500.00	400.00	100.00

Note: Exhibit assumes an average member bank reserve requirement of 20 percent of demand deposits.

Source: Board of Governors of the Federal Reserve System, 1963:73.

Exhibit 2
Summary of U.S. International Transactions, 1960–2001

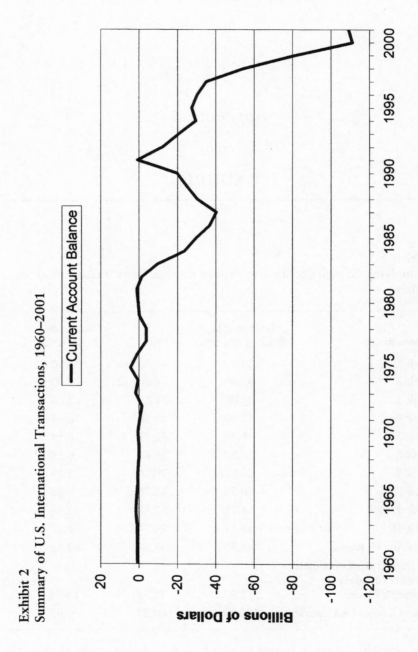

Exhibit 3
Federal Debt Held by International Investors

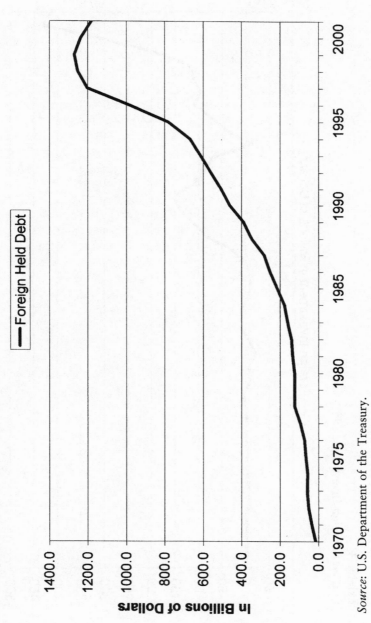

Source: U.S. Department of the Treasury.

Exhibit 4
U.S. Net Foreign Investment, 1959–2001

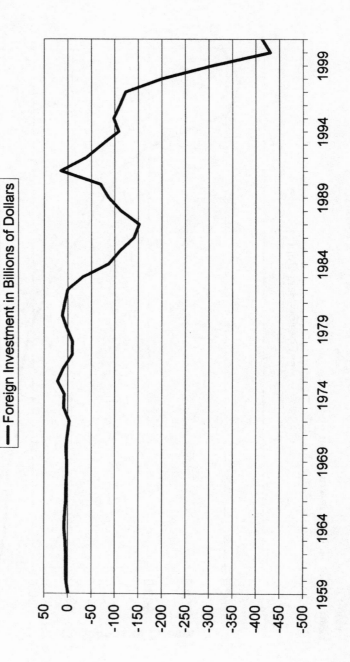

Exhibit 5
The J-Curve

Balance Worsens   Balance Improves

■ Trade Balance

Note: The X-axis represents the passage of time.

Source: Gonnelli, 1993:31.

Appendix B

The Research Design

The case study approach is the research design used in studying why some countries' policy makers actively pursue policies to create trade balances while others do not. Document analysis was the requisite data collection technique used in this design. The case study method is useful in understanding phenomena that is difficult to observe. The second reason the case study method is beneficial to this study is, as Johnson and Joslyn state,

Cases with similar environments can be chosen. Furthermore, lack of complete control over the environment or context of a phenomenon can be seen as useful. If it can be shown that a theory actually works and is applicable in a real situation, then the theory may more readily be accepted. (Johnson and Joslyn, 1995:145)

While realizing the weaknesses and criticisms of the case study approach, such as what some critics call "lack of rigor" (Johnson and Joslyn, 1995:147) (meaning the possibility of bias in the use of evidence selection), and also the potential difficulty of making the study generalizable due to the nature of policies in general (meaning the fact that they are dealing with contemporary events), the case study approach is the most prudent. As Yin argues in support of the case study approach,

Case studies, like experiments, are generalizable to theoretical propositions and not to populations or universes. In this sense, the case study, like the experiment, does not represent a "sample," and the investigator's goal is to expand and generalize theories (analytic generalization) and not to enumerate frequencies (statistical generalization). (Yin, 1989:23)

This distinction is an important one to make, particularly as the study poses the hypothesis that central banking policies (the independent variables) ultimately cause trade balances, surpluses, or deficits (the dependent variables).

The case study was conducted from a U.S. central banking perspective, with comparisons being made to the German Bundesbank. A case study approach worked nicely here because the two central banks that were examined have similar approaches in key policy areas, such as anti-inflation mechanisms, yet do not have similar trade imbalances. The reasoning for this scenario largely stems from the fact that the U.S. Federal Reserve System and the German central bank, prior to European Monetary Union unification, engaged in banking activities and policy that were similar. This comparison is interesting in light of the fact that while many of the technical goals of the two central banking institutions were similar, their respective countries' trade balances were quite opposite.

The political independence, particularly in Germany, and the strict regulatory controls that the two central banks placed on themselves, should answer those who will question the validity of such a study without including Japan, the third currency "powerhouse." Japan's economic and banking troubles have largely stemmed from banking transparency issues that were brought to light in the late 1990s. While such a study would be interesting in its own light, because of the stark differences in central banking policies, Japan has been for the most part left out of this study, with the exception of pertinent data and examples when dealing with international political economy in general. The study focused on the historical aspects that led to the establishment of a Federal Reserve System in the United States in the beginning of the twentieth century, and then moved to the latter part of the twentieth century, culminating with the establishment of the European Central Bank, which has largely taken over many of the previous functions of the German Bundesbank.

The case study approach allowed for an important analysis of two of the world's largest economic forces and currencies, the dollar and the mark, and demonstrated how the United States and Germany play major roles in the global trading society as members of influential trading blocs, NAFTA and the EU. These relationships are important to international relations because the question must be raised whether economics has surpassed or even replaced military prowess as the hegemonic indicator in the new balance of power structure.

Many scholars believe economic power replacing military strength would lead to a more peaceful world order. However, it may be quite possible that the opposite is true. As international trade grows in importance, competing trade blocs may be coerced into using military force to defend the perceived national interests, the market place. Such a scenario could very well lead to another era of imperialism, rather than peace.

Additionally, there will always be segments of the human race that will be critical of the military or economic success of other nations or groups. Whether the criticism is ideological, religious, paranoia-based, or just old-fashioned jealousy, the security threats to the nation that houses the elements at the heart of the criticism are real. Terrorists targeted the symbolic heart of the U.S. economy when they crashed airplanes into the World Trade Center, wreaking havoc on certain sectors of the nation's economy by undermining consumer confidence. They wouldn't have targeted the twin towers if they hadn't felt that economics was a source of power. They also targeted the Pentagon, the central nervous system of the U.S. military, which would indicate that this group of terrorists perceived the U.S. power to lie in both its economic and military institutions.

Another question that is raised in regard to the future of competing trade blocs is whether or not the competition for markets needs to be played out in a zero-sum game. It will be proposed that it may be possible for all countries to benefit to some extent in the international community, or that at the very least, there can be a zero-sum game where an international organization acts as a referee. This scenario would at least require all parties to abide by the same rules and would ensure a sense of fairness in the new global market system.

The next major issue that must be addressed is why this study has focused on banking, particularly central banking, when the research question deals with the issue of international trade. The reason that central banking has served as the core to this study on international trade is due to the importance placed on liquidity in modern commerce. Whereas banking has grown increasingly reliant on the stock market to obtain its assets, central banking has been perceived to be essential to any trading society. This study questions the validity of this perception and determines whether governments are acting within the national interest based on the results of the study.

One of the most important functions in banking centers around the function of balancing the asset side of the ledger to meet the liability side of the ledger. In this sense, a country can be seen as one large bank. A country that runs consistent trade deficits, such as the United States, is not keeping the asset/liability ratio in proper balance while a country that runs consistent trade surpluses is acting like a bank that is making a profit. When more money goes out than comes in, the debt has to be financed in order for the country to keep its asset reserves in line with its liabilities. This function can continue as long as credit is readily available, but continual deficits can cause investors to lose confidence, hence undermining the financial assets, which can cause credit to become tight.

The research design, a case study looked at through the lens of banking, sheds light on the larger question of why some countries actively pursue policies to create trade balances or surpluses while others do not. The overall analysis should help to support or refute the most influential theoretical paradigms in the field of international relations by further informing the debate, and that alone makes the study valid.

NEOREALISM AND INSTITUTIONAL MODEL COMPARISONS

Table B.1 has been constructed as a template to measure the characteristics of the case study to see which paradigm better explains the phenomena analyzed and whether or not the facts of the case can be framed effectively under either model. Throughout this study reference is made to each of these variables, demonstrating how many of the institutional elements are explained in the Federal Reserve case study while the neorealist elements that are found are nullified by the fact that military power would have to take second place to economic power, which is impossible under the neorealist model.

Table B.1
Competing Variables and Characteristics of Institutional and Neorealist Models

	Institutional Model	Neorealist Model
National Interest	Not necessary, but bounded rationality exists in anarchic system	Absolutely necessary; states are rational actors in an anarchic system
Military Power	Not absolutely necessary but possible	Most important variable in achieving national interest, but long-term hegemony is impossible
Economic Power	Not absolutely necessary but possible	Not first priority, but can be secondary once security interests are addressed
Institutions Matter	Absolutely	Irrelevant in larger scheme of balance of power and national interest
Cooperation	Possible	Short-term is possible if used to achieve power interests but long-term cooperation is impossible
Balance of Power	Not absolutely necessary	Absolutely necessary
Zero-Sum	Not necessary	Absolutely necessary

Notes

1. This type of transaction would probably be referred to today as a lack of transparency and has been linked, rightly or wrongly, to many of the Asian banking industry's problems.

2. A similar scenario is occurring in the world today. Investor confidence is extremely tenuous, and in places like Japan, where low-interest loans are being offered to boost the economy, no one is taking out loans, and therefore investment has slowed considerably. Even in the United States, after the September 11, 2001 terrorist attacks, consumers could not be swayed to purchase big-ticket items and corporations were slow to take out even low-interest loans because confidence in the economy had faltered.

3. "Until the First World War, the Bank of England provided a physical backing of gold for its bank notes. Only in 1971 did the United States adopt unbacked fiat money (promising prior to that time to redeem all paper currency, on demand, with its equivalence in precious metals, thus providing a *de facto* gold standard for the world)" (Cohen, 1997:12).

4. After World War I and World War II, the United States had acquired most of the world's gold reserves and this is when the United States ultimately became a hegemon in economic terms and when the dollar became the international currency it is today. For a more in-depth look see Charles Kindleberger's (1986) *The World in Depression, 1929–1939*.

5. Hobson also discusses other nation-states engaging in imperialism, such as Germany, Belgium, the United States, and Holland, but his main focus in the book is on Great Britain.

6. The argument was being made that Great Britain was not large enough geographically to support its growing population and that there were not enough occupations to support either the professional or working

classes. Hobson noted that, however, not only was Great Britain's wealth far outgrowing its population, but that its population growth was stagnant. Furthermore, Hobson concluded that the tropical lands that were being annexed to Great Britain were areas that the English would not inhabit anyway, thus completely invalidating the policy from this standpoint alone.

7. On this point Hobson actually favored free trade and thought that it could lead to better international relations.

8. Hobson notes that very little trade actually occurred with the vast majority of colonies and regions that Britain claimed in the late nineteenth century. "The distinctive feature of modern Imperialism, from the commercial standpoint, is that it adds to our empire tropical and sub-tropical regions with which our trade is small, precarious and unprogressive. . . . At whatever figure we estimate the profits in this trade, it forms an utterly insignificant part of our national income, while the expenses connected directly and indirectly with the acquisition, administration and defence of these possessions must swallow an immeasurably larger sum" (Hobson, 1965:38–39).

9. This "fourth" is the percentage of the population that Hobson asserts is living below the bare minimum standard-of-living level essential to survival.

10. These same arguments are often used now to support the privatization of many public sector functions.

11. Many of the arguments for and against the federal bank stemmed from the same values and beliefs that caused the debate between the Federalists and Anti-federalists prior to the ratification of the Constitution, namely state's rights versus a more centralized republic.

12. The agrarians continued to feel this way throughout Hammond's account. Speculators, especially during Jackson's presidency, used these beliefs to push through the self-interested decentralizing measures that effectively dismantled the Bank of the United States and separated the federal government from control of the monetary supply.

13. There is no doubt that this was a grave concern as the various bank notes that were being circulated were exchanging at different values. Senator Sherman, while arguing for passage of the new banking system before Congress stated, "There were 1642 banks in the United States, established by the laws of twenty-eight different states. . . . With this multiplicity of banks, . . . it was impossible to have a uniform national currency, for its value was constantly affected by their issues" (Hammond, 1985:726).

14. The Sherman Antitrust Act made trusts illegal.

15. One of the benefits of centralizing the nation's reserves would be that they could require banks, particularly country banks which caused seasonal problems at crop harvest time, to keep larger reserve ratios. Forcing these banks to keep larger reserve ratios would give the banks less

money to loan on call in the money market, which was a source of volatility in the financial markets. If the loans that were made on call were then invested in the stock market, once the banks demanded the money, the investors would have to sell off the stocks to pay back the loans, which could cause distress to the entire system.

16. Crisis spending, such as in the wake of the September 11, 2001 terrorist attacks, is a necessary and critical role of government. It would not be prudent for the United States to have a budget surplus while passing up opportunities to help out communities or industries directly affected by a national tragedy.

References

Arrighi, Giovanni. 1994. *The Long Twentieth Century: Money, Power, and the Origins of Our Times*. New York: Verso Press.

Bachrach, Peter and Morton Baratz. 1962. "The Two Faces of Power." *American Political Science Review* 56: 947–952.

Balderston, Frederick E. 1985. *Thrifts in Crisis: Structural Transformation of the Savings and Loan Industry*. Cambridge, MA: Ballinger Publishing Company.

Benston, George J. 1986. *An Analysis of the Causes of Savings and Loan Association Failures*. New York: Salomon Brothers Center for the Study of Financial Institutions, New York University.

Board of Governors of the Federal Reserve System. 1963. *The Federal Reserve System: Purposes and Functions*. Washington, DC: Division of Administrative Services, Board of Governors of the Federal Reserve System.

Brookings Task Force. 1989. *Blueprint for Restructuring America's Financial Institutions: Report of a Task Force*. Washington, DC: The Brookings Institution.

Broz, J. Lawrence. 1997. *The International Origins of the Federal Reserve System*. Ithaca, NY: Cornell University Press.

Cohen, Edward. 1997. *Athenian Economy and Society: A Banking Perspective*. Princeton, NJ: Princeton University Press.

Cookson, Richard. April 17, 1999. "Survey: International Banking." *The Economist* 351 (8115): 1–38.

Dahl, Robert A. 1961. *Who Governs?* New Haven, CT: Yale University Press.

Dahl, Robert A. 1969. "The Concept of Power." In Roderick Bell, David

M. Edwards, and R. Harrison Wagner, eds., *Political Power: A Reader in Theory and Research*. New York: Free Press, pp. 79–93.

Deutsche Bundesbank. April 18, 1996. *Deutsche Bundesbank Annual Report 1995*. Frankfurt am Main, Federal Republic of Germany: Deutsche Bundesbank.

Downs, Anthony. 1957. *An Economic Theory of Democracy*. New York: Harper.

Durkheim, Emile. 1964 [1893]. *The Division of Labor in Society*. George Simpson, trans. New York: Free Press.

Eichler, Ned. 1989. *The Thrift Debacle*. Berkeley: University of California Press.

Eiteman, David K. et al. 1995. *Multinational Business Finance*. Reading, MA: Addison-Wesley.

Federal Reserve Bank of San Francisco. 1996a. "The Federal Reserve System in Brief: How the Fed Guides Monetary Policy." The Federal Reserve System: Economic Information. Internet. www.frbsf.org.

Federal Reserve Bank of San Francisco. 1996b. "The Federal Reserve System in Brief: The Many Roles of the Fed." The Federal Reserve System: Economic Information. Internet. www.frbsf.org.

Federal Reserve Bank of San Francisco. 1996c. "The Federal Reserve System in Brief: The Nation's Central Bank." The Federal Reserve System: Economic Information. Internet. www.frbsf.org.

Federal Reserve Board of Governors. September 27, 1996. "Federal Reserve Board: Federal Open Market Committee (FOMC)." FOMC Calendar for 1996. Internet. www.bog.frb.fed.us.

Friedman, Milton. 1962. *Capitalism and Freedom*. Chicago: University of Chicago Press.

Garn–St. Germain Depository Institutions Act of 1982. 1982. Public Law 97–320, 97th U.S. Congress.

Gaventa, John. 1982. *Power and Powerlessness*. Chicago: University of Illinois Press.

German News Team. October 1996. "Bundesbank." German News-DE-News: Glossary. Internet. www.mathematik.uni-ulm.de.

Goldstein, Judith and Robert O. Keohane, eds. 1993. *Ideas and Foreign Policy: Beliefs, Institutions, and Political Change*. Ithaca, NY: Cornell University Press.

Gonnelli, Adam. 1993. *The Basics of Foreign Trade and Exchange*. New York: Federal Reserve Bank of New York, Public Information Department.

Gramsci, Antonio. 1957. *The Modern Prince and Other Writings*. New York: International Publishers.

Greider, William. 1987. *Secrets of the Temple: How the Federal Reserve Runs the Country*. New York: Simon & Schuster.

Greider, William. 1989. *The Trouble with Money*. Knoxville, TN: Whittle Direct Books.

Greider, William. 1997. *One World, Ready or Not: The Manic Logic of Global Capitalism*. New York: Simon & Schuster.

Hamilton, Alexander. 1850 [1791]. "Report on the Subject of Manufactures." In *Works of Hamilton*, Vol. III. New York: John F. Trow.

Hammond, Bray. 1985. *Banks and Politics in America: From the Revolution to the Civil War*. Princeton, NJ: Princeton University Press.

Hearing before the Committee on the Budget, House of Representatives. January 26, 1989. *The Thrift Institution Crisis and Its Potential Impact on the Federal Budget*. 101st Congress, 1st Session. Washington, DC: U.S. Government Printing Office.

Hearing before the Subcommittee on Government Information and Regulation, Committee on Governmental Affairs, U.S. Senate. 1992. *Various Proposals to Regulate GSEs and to Examine the Risk These Entities Pose to U.S. Taxpayers*. 102nd Congress, 1st Session. July 18, 1991. Washington, DC: U.S. Government Printing Office.

Hobson, J. A. 1965. *Imperialism*. Ann Arbor: University of Michigan Press.

Ikenberry, G. John. 1993. "Creating Yesterday's New World Order." In Judith Goldstein and Robert O. Keohane, eds., *Ideas and Foreign Policy*. Ithaca, NY: Cornell University Press, pp. 57–86.

Jackson, John H. 1999. *The World Trading System: Law and Policy of International Economic Relations*. Cambridge, MA: MIT Press.

Johnson, Janet B. and Richard A. Joslyn. 1995. *Political Science Research Methods*. Washington, DC: Congressional Quarterly.

Kaldor, Nicholas. 1982. *The Scourge of Monetarism*. New York: Oxford University Press.

Kaltenthaler, Karl. 1998. *Germany and the Politics of Europe's Money*. Durham, NC: Duke University Press.

Keohane, Robert O., ed. 1986. *Neorealism and Its Critics*. New York: Columbia University Press.

Keohane, Robert O. and Helen V. Milner, eds. 1996. *Internationalization and Domestic Politics*. Cambridge, MA: Cambridge University Press.

Keohane, Robert O., Joseph S. Nye, and Stanley Hoffmann. 1993. *After the Cold War: International Institutions and State Strategies in Europe, 1989–91*. Cambridge, MA: Harvard University Press.

Keynes, John Maynard. 1964. *The General Theory of Employment, Interest, and Money*. New York: Harcourt Brace Jovanovich.

Kindleberger, Charles P. 1986. *The World in Depression, 1929–1939*. Berkeley: University of California Press.

Kormendi, Roger C., Victor L. Bernard, et al. 1989. *Crisis Resolution in*

136 References

the Thrift Industry: A Mid America Institute Report. Norwell, MA: Kluwer Academic Publishers.

Krugman, Paul. 1995. The Age of Diminished Expectations. Cambridge, MA: MIT Press.

Labaton, Stephen. November 5, 1999. "Congress Passes Wide-Ranging Bill Easing Bank Laws." New York Times.

Lane, Robert E. 1986. "Market Justice, Political Justice." American Political Science Review 80(2): 383–402.

Lanjouw, G. J. 1995. International Trade Institutions. Heerlen: Open University of the Netherlands.

List, Friedrich. 1983 [1837]. National System of Political Economy, ed. W. O. Henderson. London: Frank Cass.

Livingston, James. 1986. Origins of the Federal Reserve System: Money, Class, and Corporate Capitalism, 1890–1913. Ithaca, NY: Cornell University Press.

Lowi, Theodore. 1979. The End of Liberalism. New York: W.W. Norton & Co.

Lukes, Steven. 1974. Power: A Radical View. London: Macmillan.

Mearsheimer, John J. 1990. "Back to the Future: Instability in Europe after the Cold War." International Security 15(1): 5–56.

Millman, Gregory J. 1995. The Vandals' Crown: How Rebel Currency Traders Overthrew the World's Central Banks. New York: Simon & Schuster.

Mills, C. Wright. 1956. The Sociological Imagination. New York: Oxford University Press.

Miroff, Bruce, Raymond Seidelman, and Todd Swanstrom. 1995. The Democratic Debate. Boston: Houghton Mifflin Company.

98th Congress, 2nd Session Vote. 1984. Debate Over Amending the Garn–St. Germain Act. Washington, DC.

Olson, Mancur. 1965. The Logic of Collective Action. Cambridge, MA: Harvard University Press.

Parenti, Michael. 1970. "Power and Pluralism: A View from the Bottom." Journal of Politics 32: 501–530.

Polsby, Nelson W. 1963. Community Power and Political Theory. New Haven, CT: Yale University Press.

Reuters World Service via Individual, Inc. September 27, 1996. NewsPage: An Information Service from Individual, Inc. Currency Markets (Banking, Finance & Real Estate/Financial Services & Investment). "Kohl Says EMU Criteria, Deadline Will Be Met." Internet. www.newspage.com.

Robinson, Michael A. 1990. Overdrawn: The Bailout of American Savings. New York: Penguin Books.

Rose, Warner. March 26, 1996. "Greenspan Says Controlling Inflation Number One Goal." Washington, DC: U.S. Information Agency.

Rossiter, Clinton, ed. 1961. *The Federalist Papers*. New York: Penguin Books USA.

Salamon, Lester and Stephen Van Evera. 1973. "Fear, Apathy and Discrimination: A Test of Three Explanations of Political Participation." *American Political Science Review* 67: 1288–1306.

Sanger, David E. February 20, 1999. "U.S. Trade Deficit in 1998 Was Worst Ever." *New York Times*.

Sbragia, Alberta M. and John T. Woolley, eds. 1992. *Euro-Politics: Institutions and Policymaking in the "New" European Community*. Washington, DC: The Brookings Institution.

Schattschneider, E. E. 1975. *The Semisovereign People*. Orlando, FL: Holt, Rinehart and Winston.

Seymour, Harold J. 1988. *Designs for Fund-raising: Principles—Patterns—Techniques*. Rockville, MD: Fund Raising Institute.

Smith, Adam. 1976 [1776]. *An Inquiry into the Nature and Causes of the Wealth of Nations*, ed. Edwinn Cannan. Chicago: University of Chicago Press.

Snow, Donald M. 1995. *National Security: Defense Policy for a New International Order*. New York: St. Martin's Press.

Subcommittee on Economic Goals and Intergovernmental Policy of the Joint Economic Committee, Congress of the United States. 1984. "The Economic Impact of Federal Deficits, 1984–1989." Washington, DC: U.S. Government Printing Office.

Tyson, Laura D'Andrea. Winter 1991. "They Are Not Us: Why American Ownership Still Matters." *The American Prospect* (4): 37–49. Internet. www.epn.org/prospect/04/04tyso.html.

U.S. Department of State. September 1996. "Brief Overview of the German Economy." German Embassy: Office of German, Austrian and Swiss Affairs; Bureau of European and Canadian Affairs. Internet. www.ncf.carleton.ca. Internet. www.germany-info.org.

U.S. Treasury: Monthly Update. January 15, 1996. "Update DM." Internet. www.treasury.boi.ie.

Waltz, Kenneth N. 1979. *Theory of International Politics*. Reading, MA: Addison-Wesley.

Weimer, David and Aidan Vining. 1992. *Policy Analysis: Concepts and Practice*. Englewood Cliffs, NJ: Prentice Hall.

Wilmsen, Steven K. 1991. *Silverado*. Washington, DC: National Press Books.

Wilson, James Q. 1975. "The Rise of the Bureaucratic State." *The Public Interest* 41: 77–103.

Wolf, Charles, Jr. 1995. *Perspectives on Economic and Foreign Policies.* Santa Monica, CA: Rand.

Wolf, Eric. 1969. *Peasant Wars of the Twentieth Century.* London: Faber and Faber.

Woodrow: Federal Reserve Bank of Minneapolis. February 20, 1996. "1996 Monetary Policy Objectives: Testimony by Alan Greenspan, Chairman, Board of Governors of the Federal Reserve System, before the Committee on Banking, Housing, and Urban Affairs, U.S. Senate, February 20, 1996." Internet. www.woodrow.mpls.frb.fed.us.

Yin, Robert K. 1989. *Case Study Research: Design and Methods.* Beverly Hills, CA: Sage.

Index

Afghanistan, 96
Agenda, 23, 67, 76, 98, 113
Agenda setting, 55, 57, 71
Anti-deregulation, 44–49
Anti-federalists, 67–68
Arrighi, Giovanni, 19
Asia, 19
"Asian Flu," 39
Assets, 18, 24–53, 102; asset portfolio, 18, 28, 50

Bachrach, Peter, 72–73
Balance of power, 13, 18, 23
Balderston, Frederick, 45
Banking, 27–53, 109–115
Baratz, Morton S., 72–73
Basle Accord, 37–38
Behavioralism, 70
Benston, George, 42–43
Bounded rationality, 56
Bretton Woods Agreement, 22, 24, 84
Brookings Institution, 43–44
Broz, J. Lawrence, 36
Brutus, 67–68
Budget deficit, 100

Bureaucracy, 74–75
Bush, George H. W., 89

Carter, Jimmy, administration, 42
Central banks, 25, 27, 30, 36
Civil War, 62
Clinton, Bill, 8, 81, 89, 100
Cohen, Edward, 35
Cold War, 16–17
Congress, 75–76
Constitution, 67–68
Consumer confidence, 30, 34, 91–93
Cookson, Richard, 37–39
Cooperation, 114
Corporate capitalists, 3, 24, 28, 31, 37, 52, 63–64, 65, 66–67
Corporate consolidation, 64
Credit, 28, 34–35, 50–51
Currency, 30–36
Current account, 7, 9, 81, 100

Dahl, Robert, 69–73
Depository Institutions Deregulation and Monetary Control Act of 1980, 45

Deregulation, 40, 42–45
Deutsche mark, 101
Devaluation, 80, 91–97
Discount rate, 88
Dollar, 8, 24, 58, 83, 90, 92–93, 95, 99, 112
Downs, Anthony, 74
Durkheim, Emile, 14, 17, 20

Eccles, Marriner, 99, 112
Economic Stimulus Package of 2002, 86
The Economist, 28, 37
ECU (European Currency Unit), 102
Eichler, Ned, 41–42
Eiteman, David, 80
Electronic commerce, 110
Employment Act of 1946, 76
EMS (European Monetary System), 97
EMU (European Monetary Union), 102–103
ERM (European Exchange Rate Mechanism), 102–103
EU (European Union), 19, 29
Euro, 103–104
European System of Central Banks, 101
Exchange rates, 30, 95
Exports, 9, 99

Federal funds rate, 87
Federal Home Loan Bank Board, 46, 48
Federal Reserve, 24, 27–30, 39, 51–53, 63, 65, 80, 84–93, 99
Federal Reserve Act (1913), 31, 65, 76, 85
Federalists, 66–67
Finance capital, 110–115
Fiscal policy, 86
Flint, Charles, 64

Floating exchange rate, 35, 84
FOMC (Federal Open Market Committee), 89
Foreign exchange rate market, 92
Foreign investment, 17, 90, 99
Free trade, 57–58
Friedman, Milton, 11–12, 85
FSLIC (Federal Savings and Loan Insurance Corporation), 40, 42–43, 46
Full Employment and Balanced Growth Act of 1978, 76

Garn–St. Germain Depository Institutions Act of 1982, 45
Gaventa, John, 69–74
GDP (gross domestic product), 8, 21, 95, 100
Germany: Central Bank (Bundesbank), 10–11, 98, 101–108; *Landesbanken*, 102; *Zentralbankrat*, 102
Glass-Steagall Act of 1933, 77
GNP (gross national product), 21
Gold, 24, 27, 34; standard, 34–35, 64, 84
Goldstein, Judith, 22
Gonnelli, Adam, 92
Gramsci, Antonio, 74
Gray, Ed, 40
Great Britain, 57–61
Greenspan, Alan, 93, 98–99, 112
Greider, William, 114
GSE (Government-Sponsored Enterprises), 48
Gulf War, 18

Hamilton, Alexander, 33, 35
Hammond, Bray, 31, 61–63
Hedge funds, 39
Hegemon: Germany, 105–106; United States, 18–19, 56

Hobson, J. A., 58–61; as "redistributive liberalist," 58–59
Hoffman, Stanley, 20, 111
Huntington, Samuel, 81

Ikenberry, G. John, 22–24
IMF (International Monetary Fund), 29
Imperialism, 57
Imports, 93–96
Institutional constraints, 111
Institutionalists, 16, 111
Institutions, 21–23, 57, 112–113
Interdependence, 20, 92
Interest rate, 25, 39, 41–42, 44–47, 50–51, 76–77, 86, 88–89, 100; management, 53, 76, 86, 98–99, 107
International: organizational theorists, 16; organizations, 16, 20, 25, 53, 111; relations, 13–14, 22–23, 25, 111; system, 13, 16–20, 23, 55–57, 71, 108, 111–113, 115; trade, 20, 27, 33, 62, 79, 83, 109

Jackson, Andrew, 62
Jackson, John H., 113
Japan, 8
J-curve, 96
Jefferson, Thomas, 62

Kaldor, Nicholas, 44
Kaltenthaner, Karl, 97
Keohane, Robert, 14–17, 20, 22, 81, 111
Keynes, John Maynard, 34–35
Keynesianism, 22, 41
Kohl, Helmut, 83, 104–105
Krugman, Paul, 12, 17, 42, 82, 90, 93, 95

Labaton, Stephen, 77
Lane, Robert, 44
Lanjouw, G. J., 102–103
Latin America, 24, 37, 90
Legislative mandates, 76
Lender of last resort, 36, 76
Liability, 45, 51
Liquidity, 89–90, 113
List, Friedrich, 33–34
Livingston, James, 30, 32, 52, 63–65
Loans, 30–32, 34
Lowi, Theodore, 76
LTCM (Long-Term Capital Management), 39, 51, 112
Lukes, Steven, 73

Maastricht Treaty, 10, 82, 104–105
Madison, James, 67
Malaysia, 110; Bank Negara, 110–111
Manufacturing, 112
Market failure, 12
Marshall Plan, 84
Mearsheimer, John, 16–17
Mercosur, 29
Mexico, peso crisis of 1994, 10, 98
MFN (Most Favored Nation) status, 109
Millman, Gregory J., 110–111, 114
Mills, C. Wright, 72
Milner, Helen, 81
Miroff, Bruce, 66, 68
Monetary policy, 9, 11; anti-inflationary, 9, 11
Mortgage, 31, 33, 42, 44–45, 47, 50–51

NAFTA (North American Free Trade Agreement), 29, 91

National: interest, 2, 5, 29, 32, 56, 93, 99; security, 9, 21
National Bank Act, 32
Neorealism, 13, 111
Nixon, Richard, 84
Nye, Joseph, 20, 111

OECD (Organization for Economic Cooperation and Development), 8
Olson, Mancur, 29
Open market operations, 89
Overproduction, 64
Owen-Glass Bill, 65

Parenti, Michael, 73
Pareto efficiency, 12
Participation, 69, 71, 74
Pentagon, 10
Pluralism, 70
Policy implementation, 29, 40, 49
Polsby, Nelson, 69
Populist movement, 63
Power, 70, 72; economic, 15–16, 20, 23, 56, 65; military, 15–16, 18, 20, 23, 56
Price levels, 33
Principal-agent problem, 47–48
Productivity, 100
Protectionism, 33, 91, 94

Radcliffe Report on Monetary Policy, 44
Rational actor paradigm, 12
Reagan, Ronald, 89
Recession, 7, 37–38, 44, 47, 85–86, 105–106, 108
Regulatory function, 36, 62
Reserve requirement, 31, 86–88
Reserves, 28, 64–65
Reuters World Service, 105
Revolutionary War, 62
Robinson, Michael, 40

Rose, Warner, 99
Rossiter, Clinton, 67–68

S&L (savings and loan) debacle, 40, 46–48
Salamon, Lester, 73
Salt Lake City, 49–50
Sbragia, Alberta, 101
Schattschneider, E. E., 72–73
Schumer, Charles E., 77
Seidelman, Raymond, 66
Senate, 68, 84, 98
September 11, 2001 terrorist attacks, 10, 90, 113
Seymour, Harold, 14
Silverado Savings and Loan, 46–47
Smith, Adam, 33, 57
Snow, Donald, 17, 20
Soros, George, 110
Standard of living, 9, 28, 60, 82, 95, 113–115
Stock, 25, 31–32, 36, 38; market, 27–28, 31, 35, 37, 51
Structure, 13, 18, 20–22, 71
Superpowers, 5, 17–19, 58, 82, 105–106
Swanstrom, Todd, 66
System theory, 13, 21

Tariffs, 33
Technology, 28
Terrorist attacks. *See* September 11, 2001 terrorist attacks
Trade: bloc, 20, 98, 105; deficit, 7–9, 34, 81–83, 91, 93–95, 99, 108; policy, 11–13, 23, 29, 59, 79–80, 82, 86, 90–91, 98–99, 107, 109–110
Tyson, Laura D'Andrea, 21

Unemployment, 11, 38, 51, 94, 98, 100, 103, 106
Unit of analysis, 4, 71, 111
Unit-level actors, 22–23

Van Evera, Stephen, 73
Vining, Aidan, 12
Volcker, Paul, 40, 85

Waltz, Kenneth, 13–15, 17–23
War of 1812, 62
Weimar Republic, 81
Weimer, David, 12
Wilmsen, Steven, 47

Wilson, James Q., 74–75
Wolf, Charles, 81
Wolf, Eric, 73
Woolley, John, 101
World Trade Center, 10
World War I, 24, 41
World War II, 24, 41, 46
WTO (World Trade Organization), 29, 113

About the Author

NEIL H. ASHDOWN is Deputy Director of the Governor's Office of Planning and Budget for the State of Utah. In addition, he teaches in the Master of Public Administration program at the University of Utah.